From Van Valkenburg to Vollick

V. 3: The Loyalist Storm Follick and his Follick and Vollick descendants in North America

By Lorine McGinnis Schulze

Table of Contents

Storm Follick the Loyalist & Esther

Storm Follick was baptised when he was two days old in Schoharie New York on 19 February 1765 in St Paul's Lutheran Church. His parents were recorded as Isaac & Maria Falk [sic]. [1]

Some time after September 1787 Storm married Esther, whose surname is not known. Many researchers and descendants believe she was Esther Sperbeck and a daughter of Jacob Sperback but there is no proof of this assertation. In fact a petition submitted by Jacob's son John Sperback includes a declaration from several commanding officers of the disbanded Butler's Rangers which states that when Jacob Sperback drowned in the Niagara River he left three children named John, Elizabeth and Jacob. There is no Esther mentioned.

Storm used the surnames Follick and Vollick interchangeably, and variant spellings were recorded in official documents. An affidavit filed with his daughter Sophia's land claim in 1837 explains that Storm's surname of Vollick is pronounced Follick and he is known as both Vollick and Follick.

Louth Township No. 4. Map No. A17 Original by Augustus Jones dated Oct. 25, 1791, copied from an original by Mr. Charles Chambers, & signed Samuel Holland shows Storm on Lot 10, Conc. II, VI, & V. Louth Twp.

Louth Twp. No. 4, Map. No. A15 (Ministry) Undated Map by D.W.Smith, witnessed by Thomas Ridout. Lot 10, Conc. 3,4,& 5. Storm Volk is also on Lot 9 Conc. 3, crossed out and reassigned to Philip Magregor, i.e. Philip Gregory. No longer there in 1812.

All those lots were assigned to Storm Vollick, on the 1791 Map and on the Undated Map. John Merach (Marical, etc) was on Lot 9, Conc. 4 & 5, with James Mirach aka Miracle on Lot 7, Conc. 4 & 5 on the undated Map. Isaac Vollack is sharing Lot 3, Conc.4 with Henry Beamer & John Cole. Map. No. A16, dated Jan. 25, 1812 has Isaac Vollock registered on Lot l, Con. III. John Marical is on Lot 4, Conc. 9, in 1812.

Storm Follick is found on a petition dated June 12, 1793 at Lincoln, signing with an X beside his name, which is rendered as Storm FOLK. The petition is listed as *"Philip McGregory Memorial to build a saw mill upon the stream on his farm up the Fifteen Mile Creek."* [2]

On October 17, 1795 a Gainsborough Patent in the Niagara District was registered for Sturn [sic] Volick, age 30, born USA, farmer. Storm received 200 acres on Concession 4 Lot 17.

To his Honor Peter Russell Esquire Adminstering the Government of the Province of Upper Canada. In Council. The Petition of Storm Follluck Humbly Sheweth That your Petitioner served as a Private in Colonel Butlers Corps, that as yet your Petitioner has only drawn from His Majesty 200 acres, most of which your Petitioner has improved. Therefore Prays Your Honor will be pleased to Grant him an additional 100 acres to put him on a footing with other soldiers of the Corps. And as in Duty Bound your Petitioner will ever Pray. Storm Folluck [his mark] Niagara 17 Jan. 1797

Storm Folk, -- 25 Feb. 1797. Barney McIntire. Lots in Louth. Entered Book – No. 12 – Lot 7, Conc 3 Louth

This is to satisfy all Persons that I – right to Lott [sic] Number Nine in the Third Consession Township of Louth and – half of Lott Number 10 in the 4th Concession of said Township. And have received no – for said lotts in said township of Louth of whcn Barney McIntire now – on. Given under my hand this 25 Day of our Lord 1797. Storm Folk [his mark] [Note that the surname Markle appears far left of this document, but portions are missing]

This is to Satisfy all Persons that I, Storm Folk do Acknowledge that I claim wright [sic] to Lotts in the 3, 4, 5 Concessions in the Township of Louth, No. 10 in the 3rd Concession improved by Barney Mcintire the -- -- John Markle the 5 by John Sagger. Signed – [his mark]

Storm Vollick, -- -- -- Re-- Dec. 1795. Lot 10, Cons 3,4, & 5. Entered in Book Lotts – page 1159. Lots 10, Conc 3,4,5, Louth

Upper Canada Land Petitions P Bundle Miscellaneous, 1789-1839, RG1 L3 Vol. 196 Petition 22

The Petition of Storm Folluck [sic] humbly sheweth that your Petitioner served as a Private in Colonel Butler's Corps, that as yet your Petitioner has only drawn from His Majesty two hundred acres, most of which your Petitioner has improved, therefore prays that your Honor will be pleased to grant him an additional one hundred acres to put him on a footing with other soldiers of that Corps. (Makes his mark) Niagara 17 Jan. 1797

Storm Folk, or Vollick. 27 Feb. '97
No 10, 5 Conc. Louth

This is to certify that I have no claim or Right in Lot Number 10 in the six Concession, Township of Louth, Home District, And that – -- -- Certificate -- -- John Sagge r-- -- 27 Day of February 1797. John Markle

Storm filed a petition for land on 6 March 1797.

The Petition of Storm Vollick of Grantham, humbly shews that your petitioner was a soldier inBulter's Rangers of which he has a discharge, that he has received 200 acres of his Military Lands andprays your honour would be pleased togrant him the raminaining 100 acres and your petitioner is in duty bound..... (standard formal ending) would be pleased to grant him a Lot in the town of Newark. Storm made his mark (X)

The envelope shows that the Council ordered his Military Land grants be completed and he was given a Warrant

To His Honor Peter Russell Esquire
administering the Government of
Upper Canada &c &c &c
In Council

The Petition of Storm Vollock
of Grantham

Humbly sheweth

That your Petitioner was a
Soldier in Butlers Rangers of which
he has a discharge That he has received
200 acres of his military Lands and prays
Your Honor would be pleased to part him the
remaining 100 acres & your petitioner as in
Duty bound will ever pray — Your Petitioner
also prays your Honor would be pleased to
grant him a Lot in the Town of Newark.

Newark
6 March 1797

               his
Storm   ✝   Vollock
             mark

Witness Ridout
h. O

33 No. 33

Storm Vollick

rec.d 7th March 97

Read 11th March 1797

ordered that his Military
Lands be completed —
The Town is refused
                    P.R.

Gave a Warrant
13th March 1797
Six Months

Entd

Entered in Land Book
B. Page 243.

In 1797 Storm is found on Concession Concession 4 Lot 17 Grantham Township, Lincoln County Ontario. The Old United Empire Loyalist List shows him serving in Butler's Rangers and receiving his Orders in Council (OIC) on 11 March 1797.

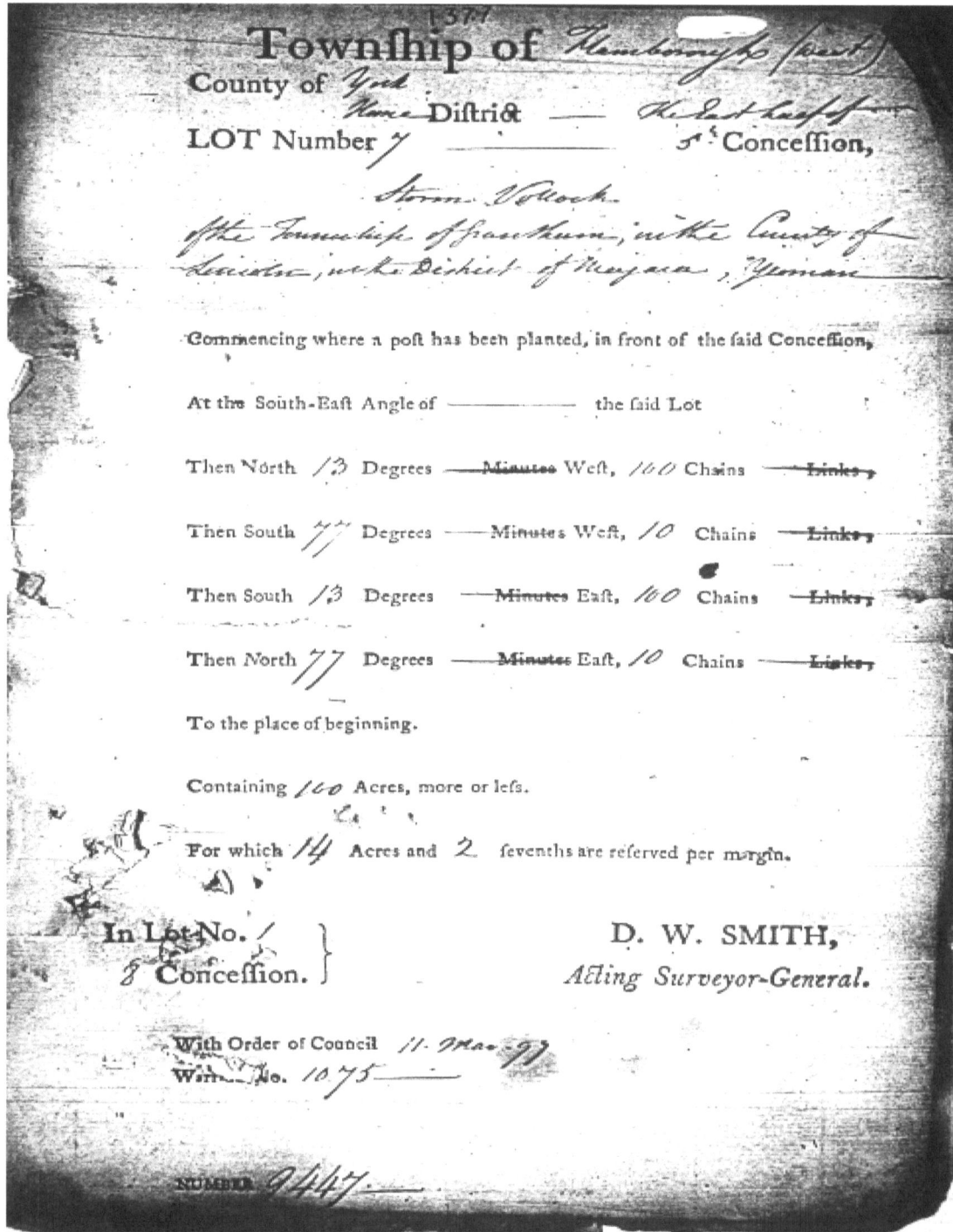

Township of Flamborough West, County of York. Lot 7, Conc. 5. Storm Vollock of the Township of Grantham, in the County of Lincoln, District of Niagara, yeoman. 11 Acres being Lot No. 1 Conc 8. With Order in Council 11 Mar 97 Warr. No. 1075.

Vollick, Sturn?.... Home District, Soldier Butler's Rangers, O.I.C. March 11, 1797

In October 1800 Storm and Esther's son Jacob was born. Since his next son was named Isaac in honour of Storm's father, it is possible that Jacob was named in honour of Esther's father.

In 1801 Storm had 100 acres on Concession 5 South half Lot 7, West Flamborough Township, Wentworth County. This land was registered 10 August 1801.

Storm served in the War of 1812 and his name is found in the Charles Askin papers. Charles was the Captain of the 2nd Regiment of the Lincoln Militia. [3] Rations allowed for soldiers' children and wives show Storm Volluck allowed 2 5/6 for his wife and seven children.

On a list "Women and Children's Names belinging to Men of Capt. Askins Company" we find Esther Volluck, Sophia, Isaac, Jacob, Peter, Catherine, Tice [Matthys] and Lena. I belive this is Nancy and not Lena.

"Township of Thorold 1793-1967" War of 1812 Muster Rolls of 2nd Registment Lincoln Militia: Private Storm Vollick in Captn Charles Askin's Co. Time of Service 26 June, 6 July [4]

Census, Canby's Settlement 1828 shows four Follick families living there.

Follick
Storm, 1 male under 16, 2 males above 16, 1 female above 16. Total 5
Jacob, 2 females under 16, 1 male above 16, a female above 16. Total 4
Peter, 1 female under 16, 1 male above 16, 1 female above 16. Total 3
Isaac, 1 male above 16. Total 1 [5]

It is likely this is the family of Storm, his 3 sons Jacob, Peter & Isaac (with families) and his son George as the male under 16. The males above 16 would be Storm himself and his son Matthias. This is evidence in support of two sons - one named Peter and another named George. It is also interesting to note that Peter has a daughter under the age of 16, meaning born between and 1812 and 1828 - which fits with Esther born circa 1824 or 1825. Jacob is the only other son with daughters under age 16 - and they are known to be Mary born circa 1824 and Elsie born circa 1826.

Vollick, Storm. Chippawa, Township of Thorold, Page: 31, 1967, Military. Welland Tribune

Children of Storm Follick & Esther

2   i.   **Jacob[9] Follick**, born Oct 1800 in Canboro, Haldimand Co. Ontario [6]died 23 Jul 1887 in Welland Co., Ontario [7]. He married (1) Rachel Smith Abt. 1823; born 17 May 1809 in Canboro, Haldimand Co. Ontario [8]; died 26 Jul 1865 in Canboro, Haldimand Co. Ontario [9] He married (2) Christian (Christina) Cramer 24 Oct 1866 in Canboro, Ontario [10]; born Abt. 1810 in Pennsylvania; died 16 Jan 1894 in Canborough, Haldimand Co. Ontario [11]

3   ii.   **Isaac Follick**, born Abt. 1801 in Ontario.

4   iii. **Sophia Follick**, born Abt. 1802 in Canboro, Haldimand Co. Ontario [12]. She married John Sperback; born Abt. 1787 in Upper Canada.

5   iv. **Peter Follick**, born Abt. 1808 in Pennsylvania? [13]; died 14 Feb 1859 in Canboro, Haldimand Co. Ontario. He married (1) Mary Labatte Bef. 1825; born in Quebec; died Bet. 1848 - 1851 in Probably Canboro, Haldimand Co. Ontario. He married (2) Ellen Crane Bef. 1851; born Abt. 1818 in Ireland; died 28 November 1890 in Canboro, Ontario.

6   v.   **Matthias Follick**, born 12 Oct 1810 in Canboro, Haldimand Co. Ontario; died 23 Oct 1879 in Canboro, Haldimand Co. Ontario [14]. He married (1) Rachel McLaughlin 1830 in Canboro, Haldimand Co. Ontario; born 26 Dec 1814 in Canboro, Haldimand Co. Ontario; died Aft. Feb 1833 in Canboro, Haldimand Co. Ontario. He married (2) Gittie McLaughlin 1834 in Canboro, Haldimand Co. Ontario; born 26 Apr 1819 in Canboro, Haldimand Co. Ontario; died 02 Jun 1900 in Canboro, Haldimand Co. Ontario [15]

7   vi. **Catherine Follick**, born Bef. 1813.

8   vii. **Nancy Follick**, born Bef. 1813. She married James White; born Abt. 1817 in Ireland; died 02 Aug 1900 in Dunnville, Haldimand Co. Ontario [16]

9 viii. **George Follick**, born Abt. 1814 in Canboro, Haldimand Co. Ontario; died 20 November 1882 in Canboro, Haldimand Co. Ontario [17]. He married Mary aka Maria (Crowley?) Bef. 1851; born Abt. 1817 in Upper Canada; died Aft. 1881.

Jacob Follick 1800-1887 m. Rachel Smith m.2 Christian Cramer

2. Jacob[9] **Follick** (Storm[8],) was born Oct 1800 in Canboro, Haldimand Co. Ontario [18], and died 23 Jul 1887 in Welland Co.,Ontario [19] . He married **(1) Rachel Smith** Abt. 1823. She was born 17 May 1809 in Canboro, Haldimand Co. Ontario [20] , and died 26 Jul 1865 in Canboro, Haldimand Co. Ontario [21] . He married **(2) Christian (Christina) Cramer** 24 Oct 1866 in Canboro, Ontario [22] , daughter of J. Cramer and Mary. She was born Abt. 1810 in Pennsylvania, and died 16 Jan 1894 in Canborough, Haldimand Co. Ontario [23] .

We find Jaob in April 1829:
Pte. Jacob VOLLICK, Age 26 yrs., Line #13, 6th Coy., 1st Regt. Haldimand Militia. LIMITS: All Haldimand County, including the settlement at Canby [ie Canborough] Rec'd 8 Apr. 1829.

1851 census Haldimand Canboro [24]
Jacob Vollick, farmer b. UC, Baptist, age 50 married
Rachel Vollick age 44
Mary Vollick age 28 single
Henry Vollick labourer, age 24 single
Frederick Vollick, labourer age 19 single [This must be Smith Frederick]
William Vollick, labourer age 17 single
George Vollick, labourer, age 15 single
Jacob Vollick age 10
Robert H. Vollick age4
Jess E. Vollick age 2

1861 Canborough Township Haldimand County Ontario Land Owners From the Agricultural Census [25]

Name	Conc	Lot	Total Acre	Cultivated Acre	Value
FOLLICK, Ellen	3	pt10	100	50	2000
SPIRBECK, John	3	10&11	29	29	600
SPIRBECK, Isaac	3	no entries--------------------------			
FOLLICK, George	3	pt10	33	33	500
FOLLICK, Jacob	3	8	139	60	3500
FOLLICK, Mathias	3	11	47	37	1400

Petition of Jacob ~~Volik~~ Vollick now of the Couty of Haldmiand, formerly of Township of Louth, Humbly Sheweth that your petitioner is the son of Storm Volik of the Township of Louth, an Enrolled U E Loyalist, is of the full age of 21 years, has taken the Oath of Allegiance, and has never had any land or orders for land from the Crown. Therefore humbly pray that your Excellency may be pleased to grant him 200 acres of the waste lands of the Crown. And permit Andrew Mercer of York to be his Agent to locate the lands and take out the Deed when completed. [more legalize] Signed with his mark in several places. Dated 10 January 1826. Witness James McLaughlin

10 July 1826. James M and Ralfe Clench declare that "Jacob Volik" is the "son of Storm Volik a U E Loyalist" and that Jacob "was too young to do his duty in defence of the Province during the late war"

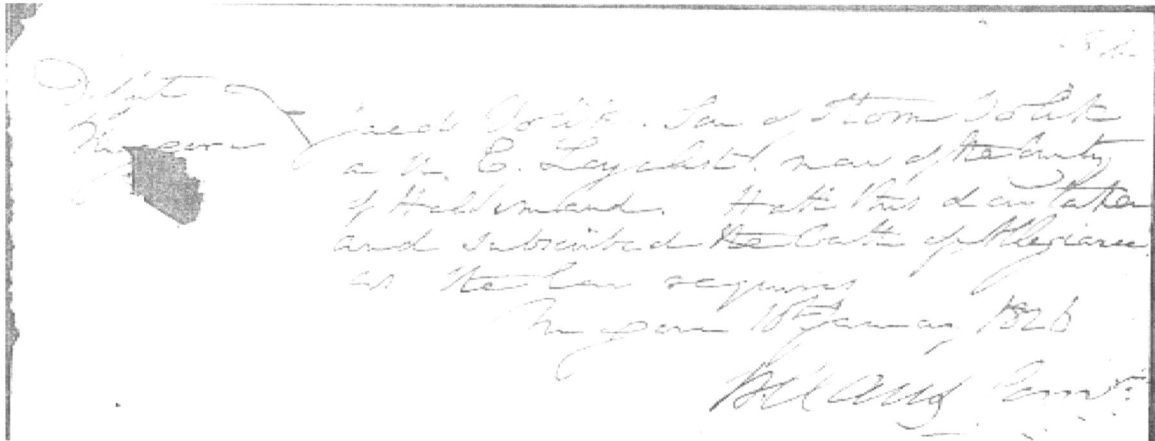

Statement that Jacob Volik son of Storm a U E Loyalist, has taken the Oath of Allegiance. 10 January 1826

<u>1866 Marriage from Haldimand Marriage Records</u>: Jacob Follick age 64 of Canboro, born St Catharines, son of S. & Hester Follick, married 24 Oct 1866 Christian Way age 54 of Canboro, born Pennsylvania, daughter of J & Mary Cramer. [26]

<u>1871 census S. Cayuga Tp. Haldimand Co.</u>
George Follick
Ellen b. 1816 Ire.,
Jacob b. 1802,
Jacob b. 1843,
Jesse b. 1844,
Mary b. 1826
Matthias b. 1813

<u>#4316 Bargain and Sale 20 March 1844 Registered 16 April 1856</u>

Jacob Vollick, Peter Vollick, Mathias Vollick and George Vollick see to William Fitch. South West Part Lot 11 Con 3, 45 acres

<u>#1570 Quick Claim Registered 1886</u>

Jacob Follick sometimes called Jacob Vollick, and wife to James H. Mellick
Part Lot 8 Con 3 46 1/4 acres and then to Smith Frederick Follick Block B. Dockstader Tract.

<u>1881 Census Pelham, Monck, Ontario, Canada</u> [27]

Jacob FOLLICK M M 80 German	Ontario Occ:	Farmer Religion:	Baptist
Christine FOLLICK F M 68 German	USA	Religion:	Baptist
Mary FRENCH F 38 German	Ontario	Religion:	Protestant

Marriage 1866: Name: Jacob Follick, Birth Place: St. Catharines, Residence: Canboro Township

Age: 64, Father Name: S., Mother Name: Hester, Spouse Name: Christina Way,
Spouse's Age: 54, Spouse Birth Place: Pennsylvania, Spouse Residence: Canboro
Township, Marriage Date: 1 Jan 1866, Marriage County: Haldimand [28]

I suggest that Rachel was a Smith, and this may be confirmed by her naming of a son
"Smith Frederick"

*The originial Homestead located on
the same property, taken my myself in
1980*

*Jacob Follick Sr & Jr inhabited the
place.*

Date Taken: 1980

Place Taken: Canboro

Owner: Dale Van Alstine

Children of Jacob Follick and Rachel Smith are:

10	i.	Mary[10] Vollick, born 25 Oct 1824 in Canboro, Haldimand Co. Ontario [29]; died 27 Mar 1919. She married William Phillmore 01 Aug 1874 in Straffordville [30] ; born 1819 in England; died 02 November 1903.
11	ii.	Elsie Vollick, born 31 Oct 1826 [31] .
12	iii.	Henry Follick, born 21 May 1828 in Canboro, Haldimand Co. Ontario [32] died 12 November 1912 in Dunnville, Haldimand Co. Ontario [33].
+ 13	iv.	Catherine Vollick, born Aug 1830 in Canboro, Haldimand Co. Ontario; died 14 Mar 1916 in Moulton, Haldimand Co. Ontario.
+ 14	v.	Smith Frederick (Frederick) Follick, born 15 Oct 1832 in Canboro, Haldimand Co. Ontario; died Bet. 1901 - 1911.
+ 15	vi.	William Vollick, born 05 Dec 1834 in Canboro, Haldimand Co. Ontario; died 10 Oct 1917 in Southwald Tp, Elgin Co. Ontario.
+ 16	vii.	George E. Follick, born 21 Oct 1836 in Canboro, Haldimand Co. Ontario; died 23 Apr 1909 in Malahide Tp, Elgin Co. Ontario.
17	viii.	Adam Vollick, born 23 Feb 1838 (Source: Family bible copied by William Oxford, Midland Ontario).
+ 18	ix.	Jacob Vollick, born 11 November 1842 in Canboro, Haldimand Co. Ontario; died 1893 in Canboro, Haldimand Co. Ontario.

+ 19   x. Robert H. Vollick, born 08 May 1848 in Canboro, Haldimand Co. Ontario; died 1911 in Manistee Michigan.
+ 20   xi. Jesse E. Vollick, born 13 Jan 1850 in Canboro, Haldimand Co. Ontario; died 07 Feb 1921 in Dunnville, Haldimand Co. Ontario.

Isaac Follick 1801-?

3. Isaac Follick (Storm,) was born Abt. 1802 in Canboro, Haldimand Co. Ontario

Pte. Isaac VOLLICK, Age 27 yrs., Line #11, 6th Coy., 1st Regt. Haldimond Militia. LIMITS: All Haldimond County, including the settlement at Canby [Canborough] Rec'd 8 Apr. 1829.

No further information has been found other than the documents below.

To *His Excellency Sir Peregrine Maitland K C B*
Major General Commander of the Forces in Upper
Lieutenant Governor of the said Province

The Petition of *Isaac Volik* ~~Vollick~~

'In Council.

of the ~~Township~~ County of ~~Township~~ Haldimand

Humbly Sheweth,

That your petitioner is the son of *Storm Volik*
of the ~~County~~ ~~Township~~ of *Haldimand* ———— an enrolled ~~U.~~ E. Loyalist, is of the full age of twenty one years, has taken the Oath of Allegiance, and has never had any lands, or order for lands, from the Crown. Therefore humbly prays that your *Excellency* ————
————————————— may be pleased to grant him two hundred acres of the waste lands of the Crown. And permit *Andrew Mercer* ———— of
Gore Dist to be his agent to locate the same, and take out the Deed when completed.
And your petitioner as in duty bound
will ever pray.

Isaac + Volik
mark

District of }
Niagara } *Isaac Volik* ———— maketh oath that he is the person he describes himself to be in the above petition ; is of the full age of twenty one years, and has never had any lands, or order for lands from the Crown.

Sworn in General Quarter }
Sessions of the Peace, this }
12th day of April }
1825 }

Isaac + Volik
mark

J. Muirhead
Chairman

District of }
Niagara } *John Doice Jun* ———— maketh oath that
Isaac Volik the above petitioner, is the person he describes himself, and has never had any lands, or order for lands from the Crown, to the best of my knowledge and belief.

Sworn in General Quarter }
Sessions of the Peace, this }
12th day of April }
1825 }

John Beter Junny

J. Muirhead
Chairman

Order in Council for Isaac Vollick aka Volik of Haldimand County, son of Storm. Dated 12 April 1825

District of Niagara. We James M and Ralfe Clench certify that Isaac Volik [sic] personally appeared at the General Quarter Sessions of the Peace, this day, is recognized to be the son of Storm Volik of Butlers Late Rangers who retained his loyalty during the late war, without suspicion of aiding or assisting the enemy' and that the said Isaac Volik was too young to do his duty in defence of the Province during the late war. Dated at the Court House at Niagara in the said District, this 12th day of April 1825

26

Isaac Volik of the County of Haldimand, son of Storm Volik of Butlers Rangers, an E. Loyalist hath this day taken and – the Oath of Allegiance as the law requires. 11 April 1825

Sophia Follick 1802-? m John Sperback

4. Sophia[9] Follick (Storm[8],) was born Abt. 1802 in Canboro, Haldimand Co. Ontario [34]. I believe she was still alive in 1871. She married **John Sperback**, son of Jacob Sperback and Margaret Coghill or Cockell. He was born Abt. 1787 in Upper Canada.

Margaret was the daughter of the Loyalist John Cockell of Butler's Rangers

> COCKELL, John of Niagara. Butler's Rangers.
>   Margaret, m. (1) Jacob Sporbeck of Niagara. Land Board Certificate
>   30/1 Beverly; m. (2) Alexander Allen.
>
> SPORBECK, Jacob of Niagara, m. Margaret Cockell. She m. Alexander
>   Allen, 6 June 1793.
>   Jacob of Niagara. OC 28 February 1807.
>   John of Beverly. OC 28 February 1807.
>   Elizabeth, m. George Upper of Niagara. OC 15 June 1820.

Source: Reid, William D. The Loyalists in Ontario: The Sons and Daughters of the American Loyalists of Upper Canada.Note that OC indicates Order in Council, which is when the land petition was read

The Petition of *Sophia Spirbeck* of the Town *ship* of *Canboro in the District of Niagara* **Humbly Sheweth:**

That Your Petitioner is the *daughter* of *Storm Follick* of the Town*ship* of *Canboro* an Enrolled U. E. Loyalist; is *married to John Spirbeck* and has never had any Lands, or Order for Lands, from the Crown. THEREFORE, Humbly Prays that Your Excellency will be pleased to Grant *her* Two Hundred Acres of the Waste Lands of the Crown, and permit *William Fitch* to be *her* Agent to Locate the same, and take out the Deed when completed—And Your Petitioner, as in duty bound, will ever Pray.

Sophia Spirbeck
her X
mark

DISTRICT OF NIAGARA. To Wit: *Sophia Spirbeck* **The above Petitioner** maketh oath and saith that *she* is the Person *she* describes *himself* to be in the above Petition, and has never had any Lands or Order for Lands from the Crown.

Sworn in General Quarter Sessions of the Peace, at Niagara this *12th* Day of *July* 1836. And I do hereby Certify that the above was read over and explained to Deponent, and that *she* seemed perfectly to understand the same.

Sophia her X *Spirbeck*
mark

Thos Butler **CHAIRMAN.**

DISTRICT OF NIAGARA. To Wit: I Do Certify that *Sophia Spirbeck* the above named Petitioner is the Person *she* describes *himself* to be in the above Petition, and has never had any Lands or Order for Lands, from the Crown, to the best of my knowledge and belief.

Thomas Butler

DISTRICT OF NIAGARA. We, *Thos. Butler* Esquire, Chairman, and CHARLES RICHARDSON, Esquire, Clerk of the Peace, do hereby Certify that *Mrs Sophia Spirbeck* who Personally appeared at the General Quarter Sessions of the Peace, this Day, was recognized by the Magistrates to be the *daughter* of *Storm Follick* who retained his Loyalty during the late War, without aiding or assisting the Enemy.

Dated this *12th* day of *July* 1836.

Charles Richardson
CLERK OF THE PEACE.

W Butler
CHAIRMAN.

Upper Canada Land Petitions S Bundle 21, 1837-1839, RG1 L3 Vol. 473 Petition 18

Order in Council dated 12 July 1836 for Sophia Sperbeck of Canboro, daughter of Storm Follick [sic] of Canboro and married to John Spirbeck. Requests 200 acres of land and that William Fitch be her Agent to locate the lands and register the Deed when completed. She signs with her mark. Thomas Butler certifies her statements are true.

(Second page of petition 18)
I certify that I am acquainted with Storm Vollick the father of Sophia Sperbeck who Pettions for a grant of land as the daughter of a U E Loyalist in hereto assured that the name of her father is improperly written in the said Petiion – entered as Storm Follick, it ought to have been Storm Vollick. Canborough August 18, 1837. Samuel Birdsall, J.P. I may further state Mr. Vollick is usually pronounced as Follick and in his own right have been written in – way.

(Envelope from Petition 18)

1851 Census Canborough Haldimand Co. p 20 C 958
John Sperback, Farmer, b. Upper Canada Methodist 64
Sophia, b Upper Canada, Methodist. 51
Moses, labourer b Upper Canada Methodist 23
James, labourer b Upper Canada Methodist 18
Mary b Upper Canada Methodist 21
John b Upper Canada Methodist 2

1861 Census Canboro, Haldimand, Canada West shows John 74, Sophia 62 with son James, his wife Eliza and their children. They are beside George Follick 46 and his children.

The 1871 census for Sophia and John's son James Sperbeck shows a widowed Sophia Sperbeck age 86 living with them. I believe this is James' mother although the age is out by a few years.

John Sperback from Beverley Township, petitoned on 25 January 1807 as the son of the deceased Loyalist Jacob Sperback. He received an Order in Council for Land on 28 February 1807. In his petition John declares that his father Jacob joined the British forces in 1783 and was a Private in Butler's Rangers. He adds that his father drowned in the Niagara River and was never added to the U.E.L. list which was the list of those Loyalists eligible for land grants. He requests that Jacob's name be added to the list.

84

To His Excellency Francis Gore, Esquire, Lieutenant Governor of the Province of Upper Canada &c ———— &c ———— &c ———— In Council.

The Petition of John Sporbeck, of the Township of Beverly, Yeoman.

Humbly sheweth

That Your Petitioner's Father the late Jacob Sporbeck, deceased, joined the Royal Standard previous to the Treaty of Separation in the year 1783, and served as a Private in Butler's Rangers until they were reduced, that some time after the Reduction of the said Corps Your Petitioner's Father was unfortunately drowned in the Niagara River, and his Name has never been inserted on the UE List.

Wherefore Your Petitioner prays that the Name of Jacob Sporbeck your Petitioner's said Father may be inserted on the UE List.

And Petitioner will ever pray

John X Sporbeck
(his mark)

York 23d February 1807

Niagara 26th January 1807

We the Subscribers, late Officers in a Corps of Rangers, Commanded by the late Lt. Col. John Butler, Do Certify that Jacob Sperback served as a Private Soldier in Butlers said Corps, and some time after the Reduction was drowned in crossing Niagara River being then Resident on the four Mile Creek Township of now Niagara, having never left this Settlement after the Corps was disbanded, He left Three Children, John, Elizabeth & Jacob all of whom have been been here ever since the death of their Father and the Two latter were born here.

Given Under our Hand

Ralfe Clench Lieut.

J.B. Ball J.P.
+ Laut. Late Rangers

Bernard Frey Capt.
Late Rangers

Thos. Butler Lieut.

Second page of 1807 Petition of John Sperback

Commanding Officers from Butler's Rangers declare that Jacob Sperback was in Butler's Rangers and that he drowned in the Niagara River leaving 3 children – John, Elizabeth and Jacob.

Land Boards of Upper Canada, 1765-1804 Jacob Sparbanks [sic]District:Nassau October 1794 Volume:6 Page(s):95 Microfilm Reel Number:C-14027 Reference:RG 1 L4 Item Number:14244

In April 1795 Jacob's widow applied for a town lot in Newark.

To —— His Excellency John Graves
Simcoe Esquire, Lieut. Governor
of the Province of Upper Canada
Major General, Commanding
the Forces thereof &c &c &c
in Council

The Petition of the Widow Sparbanks

Humbly sheweth ——

That your Petitioner is desirous
of settling in the Town of Newark, Prays
Your Excellency will grant her a Town
Lot N.o Two hundred and Seventy
Six — that she may build on the
Same — and Your Petitioner as in duty
bound will ever pray ——

Newark 4.th April 1795 ——

Upper Canada Land Petitions - the Widow Sparbanks, Newark 1795 Vol. 448   Bundle S 1 Petition 128 RG 1 L3 C-2806

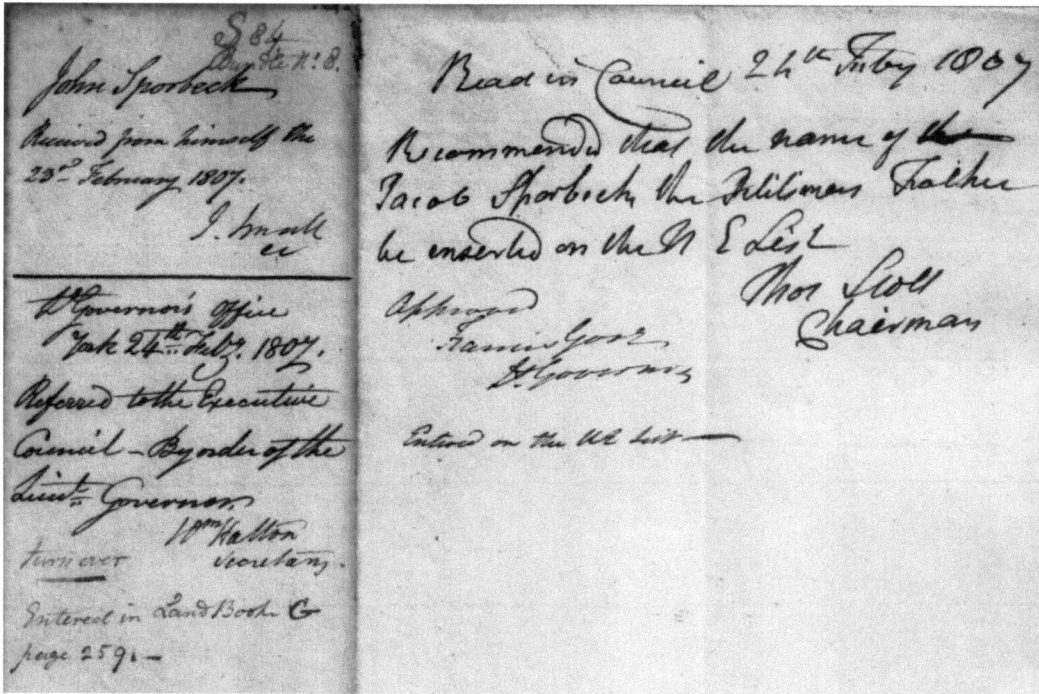

Envelope of 1807 Petition from John Sperback showing that Jacob Sperback's name was to be entered on the U.E. List

On February 25, 1807 John filed a second petition requesting a grant of land as the son of a Loyalist. He signed an Oath of Allegiance. His request was granted and it was noted on the envelope of the petition that he was to receive 200 acres of land.

85

To His Excellency, Francis Gore, Esquire, Lieut
Governor of the Province of Upper Canada &
In Council.

The Petition of Jacob Sporbeck, of the Township of
Niagara, Yeoman.

Humbly Sheweth

That your Petitioner is the son of
the late Jacob Sporbeck, deceased, an U.E. Loyalist.
That he has taken the Oath of Allegiance as will
appear by the accompanying certificate, that he
has attained the full age of twenty one years, —
and has never received any Land or Order for
Land from the Crown.

Wherefore your Petitioner prays
that your Excellency may be pleased to Grant
him two hundred acres of the Waste Lands
of the Crown as the son of an U.E. Loyalist

And your Petitioner as in duty
bound will ever pray
Jacob Sporbeck

York 25 February 1807

Turn over

95a

I do solemnly and sincerely swear before the
Holy Evangelists of Almighty God: that I
am the person I have described myself to be in
the within Petition, that I have attained the full
Age of twenty one years, and have never received
any Land or Order for Land from the Crown

So help me God

Jacob Sponbeck

Sworn before me at York in
the Province of Upper Canada
this 25 day of February in the
year of Our Lord 1807 ———
                John Small
                J. P.

I do hereby Certify that Jacob Sponbeck is the
Person he hath described himself to be in the —
within Petition & that he has never received any
Land or Order for Land from the Crown to the
best of my knowledge and belief — Witness my
hand at York this 25. day of February 1807.

                Isaac Swayze

85b

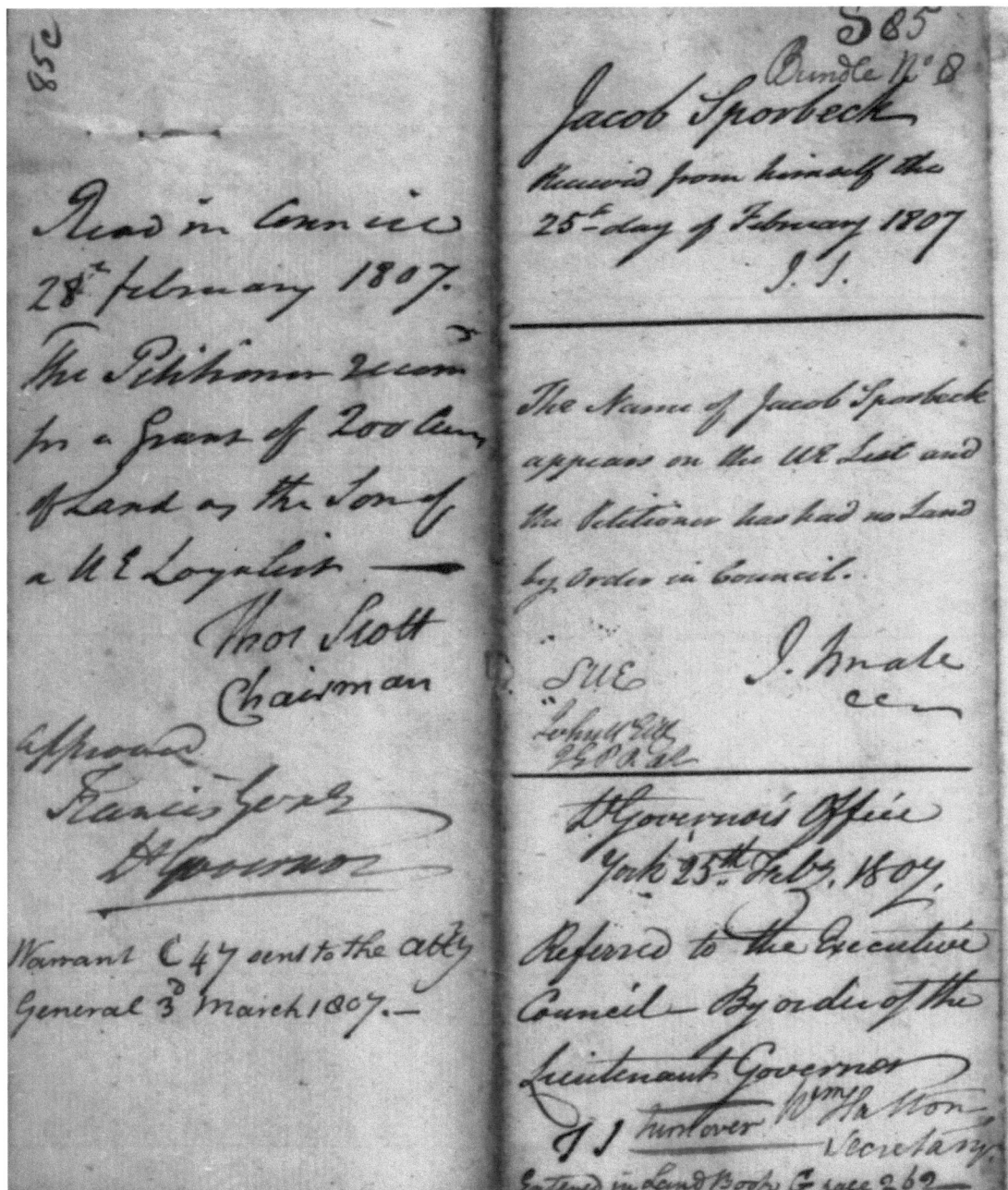

Jacob Sperback, father of John, is in "*Early Settlers in Niagara including the first 'census' 1782, 1783, 1784, 1786, 1787*" Pages 34 and 26

Jacob Spareback, 1 man, 1 woman, 2 girls [daughters], 15 acres of land cleared, 9 acres of wheat sowen, 4 people total in household [Return of Loyalists and disbanded Troops settled in the district of Niagara West from Mill Creek, Sept 17, 1787]

Jacob Sperback is listed near Jonas Larroway and Isaac Vollick on a ration list called "*List of Loyalists victualled at Niagra of Murray's District, 14 Dec. 1786*" Murray's

District is thought to be St Catharines

Jacob has 1 man, 1 woman, 1 boy under 10, total of 3 in the house

Children of Sophia Follick and John Sperback are:

+ 21   i.   Isaac[10] Sperback, born Abt. 1823 in Ontario; died Aft. 1881.

+ 22   ii.   George Sperback, born Abt. 1825 in Canboro Tp Haldimand Co. Ontario; died 20 November 1892 in Canboro, Haldimand Co. Ontario.

23   iii.   Moses Sperback, born Abt. 1828; died Bef. 1871.

24   iv.   Mary Sperback, born Abt. 1830.

25   v.   James Sperback, born 25 Mar 1832 in Ontario; died 01 Jun 1903 in Haldimand Co. Ontario [35]. He married Melinda McLaughlin daughter of James McLaughlin & Catherine Smith; born 13 November 1834 in Canboro, Ontario; died Aft. 24 Jan 1906.

26   vi.   John Sperback, born Abt. 1849.

Peter Follick ca 1808-1859 m1 Mary Labatte m2 Ellen Crane

5. Peter[9] Follick (Storm[8],) was born Abt. 1808 supposedly in Pennsylvania [36] and died 14 Feb 1859 in Canboro, Haldimand Co. Ontario. He married **(1) Mary Labatte** Bef. 1825. She was born in Quebec, and died Bet. 1848 - 1851 in probably Canboro, Haldimand Co. Ontario. He married **(2) Ellen Crane** Bef. 1851. She was born Abt. 1818 in Ireland, and died 28 November 1890 in Canboro, Ontario.

Peter Follick is found in the militia in April 1829:
Pte. Peter VOLLICK, Age 23 yrs.,Line #12, 6th Coy., 1st Regt. Haldimond Militia. LIMITS: All Haldimond County, including the settlement at Canby [ie Canborough] Rec'd 8 Apr. 1829.

#4316 Bargain and Sale 20 March 1844 Registered 16 April #1856

Jacob Vollick, Peter Vollick, Mathias Vollick and George Vollick see to William Fitch. South West Part Lot 11 Con 3, 45 acres

1851 census Canboro Tp. Haldimand Co. [37]
Peter VOLLICK, wife Helen (Ellen), and family of 9 children are found.

Peter Vollick, farmer, Upper Canada, No religion, 47
Helen Vollick, b Ireland, Roman Catholic, 32
Esther Vollick, b Upper Canada, Church of England, 23
Frederick Vollick, farmer b Upper Canada, Church of England, 17
Mary Vollick b Upper Canada, Church of England, 16
Sarah Vollick b Upper Canada, Church of England, 13
Andrew Vollick b Upper Canada, Church of England, 10
Peter Vollick b Upper Canada, Church of England, 9
Martha E Vollick b Upper Canada, Church of England, 5
John Vollick b Upper Canada, Church of England, 3
Sophia C. Vollick b Upper Canada, Church of England, 1

Next door are Matthais Vollick and wife, then George A Vollick and wife and children. Matthais and George also list themselves as "No religion"

27

To *His Excellency Sir Peregrine Maitland K C B Lieutenant Governor of the Province of Upper Canada Major General Commanding the Forces therein and therein &c &c &c*

Vollick

The Petition of Peter Volick   In Council.   County of the Township of
Haldimand District of Niagara

Humbly Sheweth,

That your petitioner is the son of *Storm Volik* of the County of Haldimand — an enrolled U. E. Loyalist, is of the full age of twenty one years, has taken the Oath of Allegiance, and has never had any lands, or order for lands, from the Crown. Therefore humbly prays that your *Excellency* may be pleased to grant him two hundred acres of the waste lands of the Crown. And permit *Andrew Mercer* of *York Esq.* to be his agent to locate the same, and take out the Deed when completed.
And your petitioner as in duty bound will ever pray.

Peter + Volk
mark

District of Niagara } Peter Volik   maketh oath that he is the person he describes himself to be in the above petition ; is of the full age of twenty one years, and has never had any lands, or order for lands from the Crown.

Peter + Volk
his mark

Sworn in General Quarter Sessions of the Peace, this 12th day of April 1825

J Muirhead
Chairman

District of Niagara } John Dour Jun   maketh oath that Peter Volik the above petitioner, is the person he describes himself, and has never had any lands, or order for lands from the Crown, to the best of my knowledge and belief.

John Buin Junny

Sworn in General Quarter Sessions of the Peace, this 12th day of April 1825

J Muirhead
Chairman

Order in Council for Peter ~~Volik~~ Vollick of Haldimand County, son of Storm Volik of Haldimand, a U E Loyalist. Peter states he is of the full age of 21 years, has taken the Oath of Allegiance and has never had any lands or order for lands from the Crown. He requests 200 acres and asks that Andrew Mercer be his Agent to locate the land and take out the Deed when completed. 12 April 1825. Signs with his makr. John Boice Jr certifies that Peter's petition is truthful.

12 April 1825. James M—and Ralfe Clench certify that Peter Volik appeared at the Geneart Quarter Sessions of the Peace on this day, is recognized to be the son of Storm Voik of Butlers Rangers who retained his loyalty during the late war without suspicion of aiding or assisting the enemy and that the said Peter Voik did his duty in defence of the Province during the late war. Dated at the Court House at Niagara.

Given Peter's wife Ellen aka Helen's age in the census records which gives her a date of birth between 1816 and 1819, it is not possible for her to be the mother of the eldest of the children. We also see an Andrew Folick listed as son of Peter and Mary at his marriage, indicating the possibility of a first wife for Peter named Mary.

Sophia C. the ninth known child, lists her parents as Peter and Ellen at her marriage. The gap of 6 to 9 years between the birth of Esther (ca 1825-28) and Frederick (ca 1834) indicates the possibility of a first wife (mother of Esther) and a remarriage prior to the birth of Frederick. Helen aka Ellen was old enough to be the mother of Frederick but not of Esther.

#4316 Bargain and Sale 20 March 1844 Registered 16 April 1856

Jacob Vollick, Peter Vollick, Mathias Vollick and George Vollick see to William Fitch. South West Part Lot 11 Con 3, 45 acres

1881 Census Canborough, Monck, Ontario, Canada [38]

Name	Age		Origin	Occ		Religion	
Normon JONES	71	Irish	Ontario	Occ: Farmer		Religion:	E. Methodist
Charity JONES	65	Dutch	Ontario			Religion:	E. Methodist
Leonard JONES	28	Irish	Ontario	Occ: Farmer		Religion:	E. Methodist
William JONES	26	Irish	Ontario	Occ: Farmer		Religion:	E. Methodist
Emily JONES	24	Irish	Ontario			Religion:	E. Methodist
Thomas JONES	23	Irish	Ontario	Occ: Farmer		Religion:	E. Methodist
John W. JONES	21	Irish	Ontario	Occ: Farmer		Religion:	E. Methodist
George W. FOLICK	12	Dutch	USA			Religion:	E. Methodist
Charity E. FOLICK	9	Dutch	Ontario			Religion:	E. Methodist

Notes for Ellen Crane:
1861 Canborough Township Haldimand County Ontario Land Owners From the Agricultural Census [39]

Name	Conc	Lot	TotAcre	CultAcre	Value
FOLLICK, Ellen	3	pt10	100	50	2000
SPIRBECK, John	3	10&11	29	29	600
SPIRBECK, Isaac	3	no entries-----------------------			
FOLLICK, George	3	pt10	33	33	500
FOLLICK, Jacob	3	8	139	60	3500
FOLLICK, Mathias	3	11	47	37	1400

1871 Census Canborough, Monck, Ontario Page 19 Microfilm reel C-9918

1881 Census Canborough, Monck, Ontario, Canada [40]
John FOLICK 32   German Ontario   Occ: Farmer Religion: E. Methodist
Andrew FOLICK   38 German Ontario Occ: Farmer Religion: E. Methodist
Ellen FOLICK 28   German   Ontario   Religion: E. Methodist
Ellen FOLICK Widow 70   Irish   Ireland   Religion: E. Methodist

Children of Peter Follick and Mary Labatte are:
+   27   i.   Esther[10] Follick, born 24 Sep 1825 in Ontario; died 1918 in Indiana.
+   28   ii. Frederick Follick, born Abt. 1834 in Canborough Tp. , Ontario; died
                 15 Apr 1884 in Wainfleet, Welland Co. Ontario.
    29   iii. Mary Follick, born Abt. 1835.
    30   iv. Sarah Follick, born 15 Aug 1835 in Canboro, Haldimand Co. Ontario;
                 died 10 November 1920 in Dunnville, Haldimand Co. Ontario [41] .
                 She married Francis Lattimore 16 Dec 1862 in Haldimand Co.
                 Ontario [42] ; born Abt. 1837 in Moulton Tp. Ontario; died 03 May
                 1906 in Haldimand Co. Ontario [43] .
    31   v.   Andrew M. Follick, born 18 Dec 1842 in Haldimand Co. Ontario;
                 died 24 Feb 1925 in N. Cayuga Tp. Haldimand Co. Ontario [44] . He
                 married (1) Elizabeth Stevens 20 Apr 1886 in Canborough,
                 Haldimand Co. Ontario [45]; born Abt. 1849 in Homer, Ontario; died
                 09 May 1897 in Canboro, Haldimand Co. Ontario [46] . He married (2)
                 Nancy J. Bloomfield 03 November 1897 in Hagersville, Ontario [47]
                 (Source: .); born 15 Jul 1870.
+   32   vi. Martha Elizabeth Follick, born Abt. 16 Jul 1846 in Canboro,
                 Haldimand Co. Ontario; died 26 Feb 1916 in Niagara Falls, Welland
                 Co. Ontario.

Children of Peter Follick and Ellen Crane are:
    33   i.   Peter[10] Follick, born Abt. 1844; died 02 Jan 1899 in Canboro,
                 Ontario [48] .
+   34   ii. John K. Follick, born 31 Aug 1849 in Canboro, Haldimand Co.
                 Ontario; died 01 November 1907 in Canboro Tp, Haldimand Co.
                 Ontario.

+ 35   iii.   Sophia Catherine Follick, born 04 Mar 1851 in Haldimand Co. Ontario; died 06 Mar 1927 in Glencor, Middlesex Co. Ontario.
+ 36   iv.   Ellen (Nellie) Follick, born Oct 1852 in Dunnville, Haldimand Co. Ontario; died 28 Feb 1926 in Tillbury East, Kent Co. Ontario.

Matthias Follick 1810-1879 m.1 Rachel McLaughlin m.2 Gittie McLaughlin

6. Matthias[9] Follick (Storm[8],) was born 12 Oct 1810 in Canboro, Haldimand Co. Ontario, and died 23 Oct 1879 in Canboro, Haldimand Co. Ontario [49] . He married **(1) Rachel McLaughlin** 1830 in Canboro, Haldimand Co. Ontario, daughter of James McLaughlin and Catherine Smith. She was born 26 Dec 1814 in Canboro, Haldimand Co. Ontario, and died Aft. Feb 1833 in Canboro, Haldimand Co. Ontario. He married **(2) Gittie McLaughlin** 1834 in Canboro, Haldimand Co. Ontario, daughter of James McLaughlin and Catherine Smith. She was born 26 Apr 1819 in Canboro, Haldimand Co. Ontario, and died 02 Jun 1900 in Canboro, Haldimand Co. Ontario [50].

We find Matthias Follick in April 1829:
Pte. Mathias VOLLICK, Age 19 yrs., Line#18, 6th Coy., 1st Regt. Haldimond Militia.
LIMITS: All Haldimond County, including the settlement at Canby [ie Canborough]
Rec'd 8 Apr. 1829.

To His Excellency Sir John Colborne,
K. C. B. LIEUTENANT GOVERNOR of the Province of Upper Canada,
and Major General Commanding His Majesty's Forces Therein,
&c. &c. &c.

IN COUNCIL.

The Petition of *Mathias Vollack*
of the Town *ship* of *Canborough* *Humbly Sheweth:*

That Your Petitioner is the *Son*
of *Storm Vollack,*
of the Town *ship* of *Canborough* an Enrolled
U. E. Loyalist; is *Twenty one years old and upwards*
and has never had any Lands, or Order for Lands, from the Crown—
THEREFORE, Humbly Prays that Your Excellency will be pleased to
Grant *him* Two Hundred Acres of the Waste Lands of the Crown,
and permit

to be *his* Agent to Locate the same, and take out the Deed when
completed—And Your Petitioner, as in duty bound, will ever Pray.

Mathias **his** x Vollack
mark

DISTRICT OF
NIAGARA. *Mathias Vollack* **The above Petitioner**
To Wit: maketh oath and saith that *he* is the Person *he* describes
himself to be in the above Petition, and has never had any Lands
or Order for Lands from the Crown.
Sworn in General Quarter Sessions of the Peace,
at Niagara this 14th Day of July 1835.
And I do hereby Certify that the above was read over and explained
to Deponent, and that he seemed perfectly to understand the same.

Mathias **his** x Vollack
mark

John Clark
CHAIRMAN.

DISTRICT OF
NIAGARA. I do Certify that *Mathias Vollack*
To Wit: the above named Petitioner is the Person *he* describes *himself*
to be in the above Petition, and has never had any Lands or Order for
Lands, from the Crown, to the best of my knowledge and belief.

James McLaughlin

DISTRICT OF
NIAGARA. We, John Clark
Esquire, Chairman, and CHARLES RICHARDSON, Esquire, Clerk of the
Peace, do hereby Certify that *Mathias Vollack* who
Personally appeared at the General Quarter Sessions of the Peace, this Day,
was recognized by the Magistrates to be the *Son* of *Storm Vollack*
who retained his Loyalty during the late War,
without aiding or assisting the Enemy.
Dated this 14th day of July 1835.

Charles Richardson
CLERK OF THE PEACE. John Clark CHAIRMAN.

Order in Council for Matthias Vollack son of StormVollack of Township of Canborough. 14 July 1835. Requests 200 acres of land. James McLaughlin certifies Mathias to be who he claims.

46

I do hereby certify that *Matthias Vollack* ——— of the Township of *Canborough* in the District of Niagara, ——— ——— hath this day taken the Oath of Allegiance to His Majesty King William the Fourth, His Heirs and Successors.

Niagara *July 13th* 183*5*, *Charles Richardson*

A Commissioner for taking the Oath of Allegiance in the District of Niagara.

Certificate that Matthias Vollack of Canborough has taken the Oath of Allegiance. July 13th 1835

I do not find that the Petitioner has received any land 24 Oct. 1835. Signature. In Council 28 October 1835. Recommended. Signatures. Warrant U. 178 – 2 Nov. 1835. Petition of Mathias Vollack 5 August 1835. Referred to the – General -- -- for the information of the Lt. Governor in Council.

1851 census Canborough, C 958 p 20
Matthias Vollick, Farmer, b Upper Canada, no religion, age 43
Gittie Vollick b Upper Canada, Baptist, age 34

George A. Vollick b Upper Canada, no religion, age 21
Catherine Vollick b Upper Canada, no religion, 19
Rachael Volllick b Upper Canada, no religion, 16
Joel Vollick, Labourer b Upper Canada, no religion, 14
Cynthia E. Vollick b Upper Canada, no religion, 12
Jesse M. Vollick, b Upper Canada, no religion, 9
Margaret S/A Vollick b Upper Canada, no religion, 8
Henry H. Vollick b Upper Canada, no religion, 2

1861 Canborough Township Haldimand County Ontario Land Owners   From the Agricultural Census [51]

Name	Conc	Lot	TotAcre	CultAcre	Value
FOLLICK, Ellen	3	pt10	100	50	2000
SPIRBECK, John	3	10&11	29	29	600
SPIRBECK, Isaac	3	no entries-------------------------			
FOLLICK, George	3	pt10	33	33	500
FOLLICK, Jacob	3	8	139	60	3500
FOLLICK, Mathias	3	11	47	37	1400

1861 census Canborough Tp Haldimand Co
FOLLICK   M. farmer, male, married, 51, born U.C. (Upper Canada), Baptist
FOLLICK   G 41, female, married, born U.C. (Upper Canada), Baptist
FOLLICK   J. 23, male, born U.C. (Upper Canada), Baptist
FOLLICK   J. 19, male, , born U.C. (Upper Canada), Baptist
FOLLICK   C. 21, female, born U.C. (Upper Canada), Baptist
FOLLICK   M. 17, female, born U.C. (Upper Canada), Baptist

May 30, 1836 & June 27, 1837: Lot 2 Conc 4, Brooke, Canborough Tp. Haldimand Co.

1871 census S. Cayuga Tp. Haldimand Co.
George Follick
Ellen, 55 b. Ire.,
Jacob, 69,
Jacob 28,
Jesse 27
Mary 46
Matthias 58

#4316 Bargain and Sale 20 March 1844 Registered 16 April 1856
Jacob Vollick, Peter Vollick, Mathias Vollick and George Vollick see toWilliam Fitch.
South West Part Lot 11 Con 3, 45 acres

#1110 Quick Claim Feb. 25, 1881 Registered Mary 29, 1881
George A Vollick & Nancy his wife
John Motley husband of Catharine Motley formerly Vollick deceased

James Warren and Rachel Warren his wife
Joel Vollick and Susannah his wife
Jacob Root? and Cynthai his wife
Jesse Mahlon Vollick Widow
Margaret Ann Vollick, spinster
Heirs at law of deceased intestate Mathias Vollick to Henry Harvey Vollick,47 acres,
Lot 11 Con 3 for 150. Block B Dockstader Tract

<u>Canboro Cemetery, Haldimand Co. Ontario</u>
"In memory of Matthias Vollick, d. Oct. 23, 1879 aged 71 years"

Gittie McLaughlin petitioned the Surrogate Court of Haldimand County in January 1880. She stated she lived Township of Canboro, was the widow of Matthias Vollick who died 23 Oct. 1879 at his residence and that he died intestate. The personal estate and effects were worth about $300.00

Gittie Vollick, Joel Vollick carpenter of Canboro Tp. Haldimand Co. and Henry Harvey Vollick of the same place, farmer, bound themselves for $600.00 to the Surrogate Court on 27 b Jan. 1880 until a full inventory is taken of Matthias' estate.

<u>1881 Census Canborough, Monck, Ontario, Canada</u> [52]

Gittee VOLLICK	F W	62 Irish Ontario Occ: Farmer Religion:	Baptist
Henry H. VOLLICK	M 31	German Ontario Occ: Farmer Religion:	Baptist
Cynthia I. VOLLICK	F	7 German	Ontario	Religion:	Baptist

Children of Matthias Follick and Rachel McLaughlin are:

+ 37   i.   George Alexander[10] Follick, born 10 Oct 1832 in Canboro, Haldimand Co. Ontario; died 23 Feb 1911 in Montpelier, Bear Lake County Idaho.

+ 38   ii.   Catherine Follick, born 17 Feb 1833 in Canboro, Haldimand Co. Ontario; died 11 May 1874.

Children of Matthias Follick and Gittie McLaughlin are:

   39   i.   James[10] Follick, born 12 Mar 1835 in Canboro, Haldimand Co. Ontario; died 15 Mar 1835 in Canboro, Haldimand Co. Ontario.

+ 40   ii.   Rachel Follick, born 1836; died 31 May 1891.

+ 41   iii.   Joel Follick, born 22 Jun 1838 in Canboro, Haldimand Co. Ontario; died 25 Feb 1899 in Lincoln Co. Ontario.

+ 42   iv.   Cynthia E. Follick, born 04 Jul 1840 in Canboro, Haldimand Co. Ontario; died 20 Jul 1916 in Pt. Colborne, Ontario.

+ 43   v.   Jesse Malon (Macon or Macow) Edwin Follick, born 08 November 1842 in Canboro, Haldimand Co. Ontario; died 05 Feb 1918 in Canboro, Haldimand Co. Ontario.

   44   vi.   Margaret Ann Follick, born 22 Oct 1844 in Canboro, Haldimand Co. Ontario. She married William Walters Aft. Feb 1881; born 07 Dec

1843 in Gainsborough, Ontario; died 26 Jun 1910 in Sarawah, Grey Co. Ontario [53] .

+ 45   vii.   Henry Harvey Vollick, born 26 Dec 1849 in Canboro, Haldimand Co. Ontario; died 28 Jun 1899 in Tillbury, Kent Co. Ontario.

Catherine Follick ca 1813-?

7. **Catherine**[9] **Follick** (Storm[8],) was born before 1813 in Canboro, Haldimand Co. Ontario,

See documents next page. Nothing further is known of Catherine.

To His Excellency Sir John Colborne,
K. C. B. Lieutenant Governor of the Province of Upper Canada,
and Major General Commanding His Majesty's Forces Therein,
&c. &c. &c.

IN COUNCIL.

The Petition of *Catharine Vollack*
of the Town *ship* of *Canborough*

Humbly Sheweth:

That Your Petitioner is the *the* Daughter
of *Storm Vollack* *as formerly*
of the Town *ship* of *Canborough* — an Enrolled
U. E. Loyalist; is *Twenty one years old and upwards*
and has never had any Lands, or Order for Lands, from the Crown—
THEREFORE, Humbly Prays that Your Excellency will be pleased to
Grant *her* Two Hundred Acres of the Waste Lands of the Crown,
and permit

to be *her* Agent to Locate the same, and take out the Deed when
completed—And Your Petitioner, as in duty bound, will ever Pray.

Catharine ☓ Vollack
mark

DISTRICT OF NIAGARA.
To Wit: *Catharine Vollack* **The above Petitioner**
maketh oath and saith that *she* is the Person *she* describes
herself to be in the above Petition, and has never had any Lands
or Order for Lands from the Crown.

Sworn in General Quarter Sessions of the Peace,
at Niagara this *14th* Day of *July* 1835.
And I do hereby Certify that the above was read over and explained
to Deponent, and that seemed perfectly to understand the same.

Wm Clark

Catharine ☓ Vollack
mark

CHAIRMAN.

DISTRICT OF NIAGARA.
To Wit: I do Certify that *Catharine Vollack*
the above named Petitioner is the Person *she* describes *herself*
to be in the above Petition, and has never had any Lands or Order for
Lands, from the Crown, to the best of my knowledge and belief.

James McLaughlin

DISTRICT OF NIAGARA.
We, *John Clark*
Esquire, Chairman, and CHARLES RICHARDSON, Esquire, Clerk of the
Peace, do hereby Certify that *Catharine Vollack* who
Personally appeared at the General Quarter Sessions of the Peace, this Day,
was recognized by the Magistrates to be the *Daughter* of *Storm
Vollack* who retained his Loyalty during the late War,
without aiding or assisting the Enemy.

Dated this *14th* day of *July* 1835.

Charles Richardson

CLERK OF THE PEACE. *John Clark* CHAIRMAN.

*Order in Council for Catharine Vollack [sic]of Canborough, daughter of Storm, dated
14 July 1835*

It does not appear
that the Petitioner
has received any Land
[?] 24 Oct. 1835

[signature]

In Council 28th October 1835

Recommended.

[signature]
P.C.

Warrant No 178
issued 2 Novr 1835

No 8

[signature]
3d [?] 1835

Referred to the
[Surveyor] General
[?] hereon for
the information of
the Lt Governor in
Council

[signatures]
S.G.
[?]
S.G.

Nancy Follick ca 1813-1900 m. James White

8   vii.**Nancy Follick**, born Bef. 1813. She married James White; born Abt. 1817 in Ireland; died 02 Aug 1900 in Dunnville, Haldimand Co. Ontario [54]

No information found that is proven to be these individuals.

George Follick ca 1814-1882 m. Mary Crowley

9. George[9] **Follick** (Storm[8],) was born Abt. 1814 in Canboro, Haldimand Co. Ontario, and died 20 November 1882 in Canboro, Haldimand Co. Ontario [55] He married **Mary Maria (Crowley?)** Bef. 1851. She was born Abt. 1817 in Upper Canada, and died Aft. 1881.

Oct 28, 1835, May 30, 1836 & June 26, 1837: Lot 31, Conc 7 Enniskillen, Canboro Tp. Haldimand Co.

#4316 Bargain and Sale 20 March 1844 Registered 16 April 1856

Jacob Vollick, Peter Vollick, Mathias Vollick and George Vollick see to William Fitch. South West Part Lot 11 Con 3, 45 acres

1851 census Haldimand Co. Canborough Twp
George 38 and Mary 34 are living in a log cabin

Next door neighbours:
SPERBACK (SPURBACH) John   Farmer 64
SPERBACK (SPURBACH) Sophia 51
SPERBACK (SPURBACH) Moses 23
SPERBACK (SPURBACH) James 18
SPERBACK (SPURBACH) Mary 21
SPERBACK (SPURBACH) John 2
VOLLICK   Peter   Farmer 47
VOLLICK   Helen 32
VOLLICK   Esther 23
VOLLICK   Frederick 17
VOLLICK   Mary 16
VOLLICK   Sarah 13
VOLLICK   Andrew 10
VOLLICK   Peter 9
VOLLICK   Martha E. 5
VOLLICK   John 3
VOLLICK   Sophia C. 1
VOLLICK   Matthias 43
VOLLICK   Gittee 34   F
VOLLICK   George A.   21
VOLLICK   Catharine 19
VOLLICK   Rachael   16
VOLLICK   Joel 14
VOLLICK   Cynthia E.   12

VOLLICK Jesse M. 9
VOLLICK Margaret A. 8
VOLLICK Henry H. 2

Names of Inmates.	Profession, Trade or Occupation.	Place of Birth.	Religion.	Residence if out of limits.	Age next birth day.	Sex.	
1	2	3	4	5	6	Male. 7	Female. 8
1 John Spraback	Farmer	Canada	Chr. Methodis'	X	64	1	
2 Sophia Spraback	do	do	do	X	57		1
3 Moses Spraback	Laborer	do	do		23	1	
4 James Spraback	do	do	do		18	1	
5 Mary Spraback		do	do		21		1
6 John Spraback		do	do		2	1	
7 Peter Vollick	Farmer	do	No religion	X	47	1	
8 Helen Vollick		Ireland	R. Catholic	X	32		1
9 Esther Vollick		U Canada	Ch. England		23		1
10 Frederick Vollick	Laborer	do	do		17	1	
11 Mary Vollick		do	do		16		1
12 Sarah Vollick		do	do		13		1
13 Andrew Vollick		do	do		10	1	
14 Peter Vollick		do	do		9	1	
15 Martha E. Vollick		do	do		5		1
16 John Vollick		do	do		3	1	
17 Sophia C. Vollick		do	do		1		1
18 Matthias Vollick	Farmer	do	No religion	X	43	1	
19 Gittee Vollick		do	Baptist	X	34		1
20 George H. Vollick	Laborer	do	No relign		21	1	
21 Catharine Vollick		do	do		19		1
22 Rachael Vollick		do	do		16		1
23 Joel Vollick	Laborer	do	do		14	1	
24 Cynthia C. Vollick		do	do		12		1
25 Jesse M. Vollick		do	do		9	1	
26 Margaret A. Vollick		do	do		8		1
27 Henry H. Vollick		do	do		2	1	
28							

#4316 Bargain and Sale 20 March 1844 Registered 16 April 1856

Jacob Vollick, Peter Vollick, Mathias Vollick and George Vollick see to William Fitch. South West Part Lot 11 Con 3, 45 acres

1861 Canborough Twp. Haldimand Co. Land Owners re Agricultural Census [56]

Name	Concession	Lot	Acres	Cultivated	Value
FOLLICK, Ellen	3	pt10	100	50	2000
SPIRBECK, John	3	10, 11	29	29	600
SPIRBECK, Isaac	3	-	-	-	-

FOLLICK, George	3	Pt 10	33	33	500
FOLLICK, Jacob	3	8	139	60	3500
FOLLICK, Mathias	3	11	47	37	1400

1861 census Haldimand Co. Canborough Tp (M=Male. F=Female)

```
21 28 FOLLICK    E.      farmer  IRE   RC   40    F     W
21 29 FOLLICK    A.      labourer  UC  none  20   M     S
21 30 FOLLICK    P.      labourer    none  18   M    S
21 31 FOLLICK    J.      UC    none         12   M
21 32 FOLLICK    S.  UC     none        10    F
21 33 FOLLICK    E.  UC     none       9    F
21 34 WILCOCKS   R.  farmer  UC     EM   30   M     M
21 35 WILCOCKS   C.  UC      EM          29   F     M
21 36 WILCOCKS   W.  UC      none        5    M
21 37 WILCOCKS   J.  UC      none        3    M
21 38 SPIRBECK   I.  farmer  US   none   74   M     M
21 39 SPIRBECK   L.  UC      EM          62   F     M
21 40 SPIRBECK   J.  labourer  UC  none       28   M    M
21 41 SPIRBECK   E.  UC      none        22   F     M
21 42 SPIRBECK   I.  UC      none        6    M
21 43 SPIRBECK   M.  UC      none        5    F
21 44 SPIRBECK   W.  UC      none        3    M
21 45 SPIRBECK   S.  UC      none        1    F
21 46 FOLLICK    G.      farmer  UC   none   46   M     M
21 47 FOLLICK    M.  UC      none        30   F     M
21 48 FOLLICK    I.  UC      none        7    M
21 49 FOLLICK    I.  UC      none        4    M
21 50 FOLLICK    P.  UC      none        2M
```

To This Excellency Sir John Colborne,

K. C. B. LIEUTENANT GOVERNOR of the Province of Upper Canada, and Major General Commanding His Majesty's Forces Therein, &c. &c. &c.

IN COUNCIL.

The Petition of *George Vollack* of the Town *ship* of *Canborough* — **Humbly Sheweth:**

That Your Petitioner is the *Son* of *Storm Vollack* of the Town *ship* of *Canborough* — an Enrolled U. E. Loyalist; is *Twenty one years old and upward* and has never had any Lands, or Order for Lands, from the Crown THEREFORE, Humbly Prays that Your Excellency will be pleased to Grant *him* Two Hundred Acres of the Waste Lands of the Crown, and permit

to be *his* Agent to Locate the same, and take out the Deed when completed—And Your Petitioner, as in duty bound, will ever Pray.

his
George ✕ Vollack
mark

DISTRICT OF NIAGARA. To Wit: *George Vollack* **The above Petitioner** maketh oath and saith that *he* is the Person *he* describes *himself* to be in the above Petition, and has never had any Lands or Order for Lands from the Crown.

Sworn in General Quarter Sessions of the Peace, at Niagara this *14* Day of *July* 1835. And I do hereby Certify that the above was read over and explained to Deponent, and that *he* seemed perfectly to understand the same.

his
George ✕ Vollack
mark

John Clark

CHAIRMAN.

DISTRICT OF NIAGARA. To Wit: I Do Certify that *George Vollack* the above named Petitioner is the Person *he* describes *himself* to be in the above Petition, and has never had any Lands or Order for Lands, from the Crown, to the best of my knowledge and belief.

James McLaughlin

DISTRICT OF NIAGARA. We, *John Clark* Esquire, Chairman, and CHARLES RICHARDSON, Esquire, Clerk of the Peace, do hereby Certify that *George Vollack* who Personally appeared at the General Quarter Sessions of the Peace, this Day, was recognized by the Magistrates to be the *Son* of *Storm Vollack* who retained his Loyalty during the late War, without aiding or assisting the Enemy.

Dated this *14* day of *July* 1835.

Chas. Richardson
CLERK OF THE PEACE. *John Clark* CHAIRMAN.

Order in Council for George Vollack [sic] of Canborough, son of Storm, dated 14 July 1835

1871 census S. Cayuga Tp. Haldimand Co. George Follick along with Ellen b. 1816
Ire., Jacob b. 1802, Jacob b. 1843, Jesse b. 1844, Mary b. 1826 and Matthias b. 1813

1881 Census Canborough, Monck, Ontario, Canada [57]

George FOLLICK	M	M	65	German	Ontario	Occ: Farmer	Religion: C. Methodist
Mary M. FOLLICK	F	M	50	English	Ontario		Religion: C. Methodist
Peter FOLLICK		M	21	German	Ontario	Occ:Farmer	Religion: C. Methodist
Isaac FOLLICK		M	24	German	Ontario	Occ:Labourer	Religion: C. Methodist
Joseph FOLLICK		M	20	German	Ontario	Occ:Labourer	Religion: C. Methodist

#1110 Quick Claim Feb. 25, 1881 Registered Mary 29, 1881
George A Vollick & Nancy his wife
John Motley husband of Catharine Motley formerly Vollick deceased
James Warren and Rachel Warren his wife
Joel Vollick and Susannah his wife
Jacob Root? and Cynthia his wife
Jesse Mahlon Vollick Widow
Margaret Ann Vollick, spinster
Heirs at law of deceased intestate Mathias Vollick to Henry Harvey Vollick, 47 acres,
Lot 11 Con 3 for 150. Block B Dockstader Tract

#1297 Bargain and Sale [after November. 1882]

Mary Maria Vollick
John Stome?? [Storm] Vollick and wife
Isaac Hartman Vollick
Peter Mathias Vollick
Joseph William Vollick
Heirs of the late George Vollick deceased to Joel Vollick
Lot 3, 55 acres Clement Tract for $500

Children of George Follick and Mary (Crowley?) are:
+ 46   i.   John Storm (Storm?)[10] Follick, born 08 Oct 1850 in Canboro,
              Haldimand Co, Ontario; died 04 Jun 1928 in Dunnville, Haldimand
              Co. Ontario.
  47   ii.   Isaac Hartman Follick, born Abt. 1857 in Ontario; died Aft. 1881.
  48   iii. Peter Matthias Follick, born 05 Sep 1862 in Ontario; died Aft. 1881.
  49   iv.   Joseph William Follick, born Aft. 1862 in Ontario; died Aft. 1881.

Schedule C.—DEATHS.

County of *Haldimand*   Division of *Canboro*

	No. 7 ✗	No. 8 ✗
Name and Surname of Deceased.	George Follick	Sarah Birdsall
When died.	20th Nov 1882	18th Dec 1882
Sex—Male or Female.	M	F.
Age.	68 years	86 years
Rank or Profession.	Farmer	
Where Born.	Ontario	
Certified cause of Death, and duration of Illness.	✓	✓
Name of Physician, if any.		Dr. A. J. Adams M. H. M. Birdsall
Signature, description and residence of Informant.	Isaac Follick Canboro	Canboro
When Registered.	30th Dec 1882	30th Dec 1882
Religious Denomination of Deceased.	Methodist	Baptist
Signature of Registrar.	Elgin Birdsall	Elgin Birdsall
REMARKS.	065951	065965

Ontario, Canada, Deaths, 1869-1938 and Deaths Overseas, 1939-1947

Grandchildren of Storm & Esther Follick

13. Catherine[10] Vollick (Jacob[9] Follick, Storm[8],) was born Aug 1830 in Canboro, Haldimand Co. Ontario [58] , and died 14 Mar 1916 in Moulton, Haldimand Co. Ontario [59] . She married **Henry Mellick**. He was born 12 Mar 1825 in Canboro Tp, Haldimand Co. Ontario, and died 22 Mar 1914 in Canboro Tp, Haldimand Co. Ontario.

Notes for Catherine Vollick:
1881 CensusWainfleet, Monck, Ontario, Canada [60]

Andrew MELICK	M M	49 German	Ontario		Occ:	Farmer	
	Religion: C. Methodist						
Catherine MELICK	F M	41 German	Ontario		Religion:	C. Methodist	
Annie MELICK	F	22 German	Ontario		Religion:	C. Methodist	
Rachel MELICK	F	18 German	Ontario		Religion:	C. Methodist	
Melissa MELICK	F	11 German	Ontario		Religion:	C. Methodist	
Hannah BRADSHAW	F 65	German	Ontario		Religion:	C. Methodist	
Richard FARRM	42	Ontario	Occ: Farmer		Religion:	C. Methodist	
Hulda FARR	F	M	40	Ontario	Religion:	C. Methodist	
Edward FARRM		18	Ontario	Religion:	C. Methodist		
Martha FARR	F	16	Ontario	Religion:	C. Methodist		
Mary FARR	F	14	Ontario	Religion:	C. Methodist		
William FARRM		12	Ontario	Religion:	C. Methodist		
John FARR	M	5	Ontario	Religion:	C. Methodist		
Francis FARR	M	3	Ontario	Religion:	C. Methodist		
Emma FARR	F	1	Ontario	Religion:	C. Methodist		
Almer FARR	M 1	Ontario Religion:C. Methodist Born:			Dec; 4 months old			

1881 Census Place: Canborough, Monck, Ontario, Canada [61]

Henry MELICK M M	56	German	OntarioOcc:	Farmer Religion:Baptist	
Catherine MELICK	F M	49	German	Ontario Religion:	Baptist
Wm A. MELICK M	26	German	Ontario Occ:	Farmer Religion: Baptist	
Henry MCGUIRE	M	10	German	Ontario	Religion:Baptist

Children of Catherine Vollick and Henry Mellick are:

50   i.   Mary Emily[11] Mellick, born Abt. 1851 in Canboro, Haldimand Co, Ontario. She married Owen McGuire 06 Jan 1870 in Haldimand Co. Ontario.

51   ii.   James Henry Mellick, born Abt. 1854 in Canboro Township, Haldimand Co. Ontario. He married Maggie Lynch 15 May 1912 in Haldimand Co. Ontario; born Abt. 1858 in Canboro Township, Haldimand Co. Ontario.

14. Smith Frederick (Frederick)[10] Follick (Jacob[9], Storm[8],) was born 15 Oct 1832 in Canboro, Haldimand Co. Ontario [62] , and died Bet. 1901 - 1911. He married

Mary Jane Varey 24 Dec 1857 in Haldimand Co. Ontario [63] , daughter of John Varey. She was born 27 Jul 1837 in Canboro, Haldimand Co. Ontario, and died 15 Oct 1914 in Canboro, Haldimand Co. Ontario [64] .

Notes for Smith Frederick (Frederick) Follick:
<u>1871 census Norfolk Co. Middleton Tp. Ontario</u>
Page 90, line 14
Vollick, Frederick, age 38, b. Ontario, Baptist. German origin, labourer
Mary age 33, English origin
John age 10 b. Ontario
Edward age 3 b. Ontario
Robert 8/12 July b. Ontario
Mary 8 b. Ontario
Rachel A. 6 b. Ontario
Living Conc 3 Lot 17

<u>#1570 Quick Claim Registered 1886</u>
Jacob Follick sometimes called Jacob Vollick and wife to James H. Mellick Part Lot 8 Con 3 46 1/4 acres and then to Smith Frederick Follick Block B. Dockstader Tract.

<u>1881 Census Canborough, Monck, Ontario, Canada</u> [65]

Fredrick FOLLICK M M 48		German	Ontario	Occ: Labourer	Religion:Baptist
Mary Jane FOLLICK F M	43	English	Ontario		Religion:Baptist
Rachel Ann FOLLICK F	16	German	Ontario		Religion:Baptist
Henry E. FOLLICK M	14	German	Ontario		Religion:Baptist
Robert V. FOLLICK M	11	German	Ontario		Religion:Baptist
James A. FOLLICK M	7	German	Ontario		Religion:Baptist
Sidney R. FOLLICK M	5	German	Ontario		Religion:Baptist

Emma J. FOLLICK   F 1 German   Ontario Religion:Baptist Born:May; 11 months old

<u>1901 Census CanboroughHALDIMAND & MONCK, Ontario (#67)</u> [66]

25   7 Follick Fredrick M   Head M Oct 28 1832 68
26   7 Follick Mary J F   Wife M Jul 27 1837 63
27   7 Follick James A M   Son S Jul 22 1874 26
28   7 Follick Alex M   Son S Mar 1 1889 11

<u>Detroit Border Crossings and Passenger and Crew Lists, 1905-1957</u> [67]
Name: Russell Vernon Follick
Arrival Date: 1 November 1928
Age: 19
Birth Date: abt 1909
Birthplace: Canboro Ont
Gender: Male
Race/Nationality: English

Port of Arrival: Detroit, Michigan
Departure Contact: Uncle James Follick
Arrival Contact: Friend Orland Houser

Notes for Mary Jane Varey:
<u>1911 Census of Canborough, Haldimand, Ontario Canada</u>
Name: Mary J Vollick
Gender: Female
Marital Status: Widowed
Age: 73
Birth Date: Jul 1838
Birthplace: Ontario
Family Number: 49
Relation to Head of House: Head
Tribal: German
District Number: 75
Sub-District Number: 1
Page: 4
<u>Household Members: Name Age</u>
Mary J Vollick 73
John Alison 18 single, domestic

<u>See Photo Mary Jane Varey courtesy Robert Shaffer on Photographs section</u>
"to Walt from ant Rachell here is gramma ant rachell jean jimmie and jimmies wife
his hired boy and uncle sydneys wife" - written on back of photo
> *People in photo*
> *Name: James Follick*
> *Name: Rachell Jean Follick (Warren)*
> *Name: Jimmies wife Almeada? ?*
> *Name: Uncle Sydneys wife? ?*
> *Name: Hired boy ?*
> *Name: Mary Jane Vollick (Varey)*
> *Name: Possible? Smith Fred Vollick*

Children of Smith Follick and Mary Varey are:

+	52	i.	John William[11] Follick, born 26 Feb 1862; died Aft. 1930 in Niagara Falls, New York?.
+	53	ii.	Mary Catharine Follick, born 27 Feb 1863.
+	54	iii.	Rachel Anne Follick, born Abt. 1868 in Canboro, Haldimand Co, Ontario; died 1953.
	55	iv.	Henry Edward (Edward) Follick, born 10 Dec 1869 in Tilsonburg Ontario [68]; died 1936 [69]. He married Almetta Rew 22 Jan 1894 in Niagara Falls Welland Co. Ontario [70] (Source: .); born 06 November 1869 in Canboro Tp Ontario; died 1954 [71].

56	v.	Robert Vernon Follick, born Jul 1870 in Canboro, Haldimand Co. Ontario [72]; died 19 Feb 1885 in Haldimand Co. Ontario [73].
+ 57	vi.	James Augustus Frederick Follick, born 22 Jul 1873; died 1944.
+ 58	vii.	Sydney Russell Follick, born 31 Oct 1876 in Haldimand Co. Ontario; died 13 Mar 1958.
59	viii.	Emma Follick, born 21 Apr 1880; died Aft. 1901.
60	ix.	Charles Haun Follick, born 1882 in Canboro, Haldimand Co. Ontario; died of scarlet fever 30 Oct 1884 in Canboro, Haldimand Co. Ontario
61	x.	Alexander Follick, born 01 Mar 1889 in Niagara Falls, Welland Co. Ontario.

15. William[10] Vollick (Jacob[9] Follick, Storm[8],) was born 05 Dec 1834 in Canboro, Haldimand Co. Ontario [74], and died 10 Oct 1917 in Southwald Tp, Elgin Co. Ontario [75]. He married **Anna Jane Smith** Bef. 1866. She died Bef. 1911.

Notes for William Vollick:
1901 Census S. Dorchester Div 2 p 11
William Follick, head, b 13 Apr 1873 Ont
Margaret, wife, b 2 Apr. 1880 Ont
William, lodger, b 3 Dec 1834 Ont
Alvero, lodger b 17 June 1877 Ont

1911 Census - see son George Alvero

Children of William Vollick and Anna Smith are:
62	i.	Viola L.[11] Vollick, born 26 Jul 1866.
63	ii.	Lydia Aldwiloa Vollick, born Bef. 1871; died 07 Jan 1871.
+ 64	iii.	William H. Follick, born Abt. 1874 in Mapleton, Ontario.
+ 65	iv.	George Alvero Vollick, born Jun 1877 in Yarmouth Tp, Elgin County Ontario; died 1962 in Aylmer, Elgin Co. Ontario.

16. George E.[10] Follick (Jacob[9], Storm[8],) was born 21 Oct 1836 in Canboro, Haldimand Co. Ontario [76], and died 23 Apr 1909 in Malahide Tp, Elgin Co. Ontario (Source: Ontario, Canada Deaths, 1869-1932 Elgin 1909, no cause of death given.). He married **Lydia Ann Smith**. She was born Abt. 1831 in Upper Canada, and died 23 Dec 1883.

1861 census Cayuga Tp Haldimand Co
BURKHOLDER	Elizabeth		CW	PM	17 F
VOLLICK	George	Laborer	CW	Bapt	21 M M
VOLLICK	Liddy	Laborer	CW	Baptist	26 F M
VOLLICK	E. G.	Laborer [sic]	CW	Baptist	2 M
SMITH	William H.	Laborer	CW	Baptist	27 M

1871 census Elgin County, Bayham Tp, E3, p 49
Range 7 Lot Pt 128 N7R 100 Acres

FOLLICK George 34, Baptist, German origin, farmer
Lydia A 35, English origin
Ephraim 12
William [H?] 9
Effie [R?] 6
Jacob 3

1881 Census Malahide, Elgin East, Ontario, Canada [77]

Geo. FOLLICK M	M	44	German Ontario Occ:Joiner	Religion:Baptist	
Lydia A. FOLLICK F	M	48	English Ontario	Religion:	Baptist
Ephraim FOLLICK	M 22		English Ontario Occ: Cheese Maker	Religion:	Baptist
Wm H. FOLLICK	M	19	English Ontario	Religion:	Baptist
Effa FOLLICK F		16	English Ontario	Religion:	Baptist
Jacob FOLLICK M		13	English Ontario	Religion:	Baptist
Etta J. FOLLICK F		10	English Ontario	Religion:	Baptist

1901 Census Ontario ELGIN (East/Est) (#57) Subdistrict: Aylmer (Town/Ville) [78]
Follick George M Head W Jun 20 1835 65
Follick Jacob C M Son M Sep 19 1869 31
Follick Martha J F Dau in law M Aug 27 1879 26

Ontario Marriage Record
James SMITH, 37, widower, railroader, Simcoe Ont., Niagara Falls South, s/o David
SMITH & Mary Ann MAYO, married Ella FOLLICK, 24, Canboro, Niagara Falls South,
d/o Storm FOLLICK & unknown, witn: George McCLELLAN & Dora REDPATH, both
of Niagara Falls South, 15 November 1903 at Niagara Falls South [79]

Index to the Aylmer Express newspaper Aug. 1907 - 1909
April 29, 1909, Page 1, c5   Died - George FOLLICK, Jaffa, age 72

Children of George Follick and Lydia Smith are:

+ 66   i.   George Ephraim[11] Follick, born 14 Mar 1859 in Ontario; died 21 Dec
              1937.
+ 67   ii. Effie Follick, born Abt. 1865; died Aft. 21 Dec 1938.
  68   iii. Charles Jacob (Jacob) Follick, born 19 Sep 1869 in Elgin Co. Ontario;
              died 1948. He married Martha J.; born 27 Aug 1879; died 1948.
+ 69   iv. William Henry Follick, born 15 Feb 1869 in Canboro, Haldimand Co.
              Ontario; died 10 November 1933 in Elgin Co. Ontario.
+ 70   v.   Etta Jane Follick, born Abt. 1872 in Straffordville Ontario; died Aft.
              21 Dec 1938.

18. Jacob[10] Vollick (Jacob[9] Follick, Storm[8],) was born 11 November 1842 in
Canboro, Haldimand Co. Ontario [80] , and died 1893 in Canboro, Haldimand Co.
Ontario. He married **Hannah Ellen Haun**, daughter of John Haun and Nancy. She

was born 04 Mar 1849 in Alymer, Elgin Co. , Ontario, and died 15 May 1921 in Buffalo, Erie Co. New York.

1881 Census Canborough, Monck, Ontario, Canada [81]

	Sex	Marr	Age	Origin	Birthplace		
Jacob VOLICK	M	M	37	Dutch	Ontario	Occ: Carpenter	Religion:Baptist
Hannah VOLICK	F	M	31	Dutch	Ontario		Religion:Baptist
Robertha C. VOLICK	F		11	Dutch	Ontario		Religion:Baptist
Agness J. VOLICK	F		5	Dutch	Ontario		Religion:Baptist

#1570 Quick Claim Registered 1886 Jacob Follick sometimes called Jacob Vollick and wife to James H. Mellick Part Lot 8 Con 3 46 1/4 acres and then to Smith Frederick Follick Block B. Dockstader Tract.

Jacob Follick Jr was born 11 November 1842 in Camborough, Haldimand, Ontario, Canada, and died 1893 in Camborough, Haldimand, Ontario, Canada. He married Hannah Ellen Haun in Ontario, Canada, daughter of John Haun and Nancy Handy.

Notes for Hannah Ellen Haun:
1900 Census 25 WD Buffalo, Erie Co. New York, [82] #53 Niagara Street
GIFFORD, Albert G. b May 1867 Canada, 33, married 11 years, immigrated 1893, PA (papers of naturalization begun), granite and Marble Cutter
-- Bertha E., wife, b Aug. 1869 Canada, 30
-- Asa B., son b May 189? Canada, age illegible
FOLLICK, Hannah E., mother in law, b Apr 1850 Canada, 50, widow, 4 children, 3 alive, imm. 1893 parents b. Eng
COLLEY, Agnes, Sister in law b Dec. 1878, 23 m 11 mos
FOLLICK, Edith M. Sister in law b November. 1886 Canada, 13
All born Canada, all immigrated 1893

1910 Census 8 WD Buffalo, Erie Co. New York [83]
Follick, Hanna H. widow, 61, b Canada 5 children, 3 living, imm. 1892 mother b Eng father b New York imm 1892
Follick Agnes J., dau. 35
Tobin Archie son in law 23 m1, zero children b New York
Tobin Edith dau, 23
Gifford, Albert, son in law, 45 m1 NAT. imm 1892
Gifford, Bertha C, dau, 41 b Canada
Gifford, Blake, son 19 NAT
Gifford, Joe, cousin 23
Gifford, Corinne, ?, 19 b New York m 1

Children of Jacob Vollick and Hannah Haun are:
+ 71   i. Robertha (Bertha) Clarissa[11] Follick, born 21 Aug 1868 in Canborough, Haldimand Co. Ontario; died 01 Jul 1944 in Buffalo, Erie Co. New York.

72	ii.	Agnes Janet Follick, born 31 Dec 1875 in Canborough, Haldimand Co. Ontario; died 29 Jun 1938 in Buffalo, Erie Co. New York. She married (1) Lewis Cooley 07 Jun 1899 in Buffalo, Erie Co. New York. She married (2) Emerson B. Howes Aft. 1915.
73	iii.	Charles T. Follick, born 22 Apr 1883 in Canborough, Haldimand Co. Ontario; died 20 Oct 1884 in Canborough, Haldimand Co. Ontario.
+ 74	iv.	Edith Maude Follick, born 17 November 1886 in Canborough, Haldimand Co. Ontario; died 01 Mar 1968 in Kenmore, Erie, New York.

19. Robert H.[10] Vollick (Jacob[9] Follick, Storm[8],) was born 08 May 1848 in Canboro, Haldimand Co. Ontario [84], and died 1911 in Manistee Michigan [85]. He married **Mary Chambers** 05 Jul 1874 in Mapleton, Yarmouth Twp, Elgin Co. [86], daughter of Daedelus Chambers and Martha Wooley. She was born Jul 1852 in Canada, and died 1891 in Manistee Michigan [87].

Notes for Robert H. Vollick:
Ontario Marriage Registration
Name: Mary Chambers
Birth Place: Dorcheshire
Age: 22
Father Name: Daedalus Charles Martha J Chambers
Mother Name: Chambers
Estimated Birth Year: abt 1852
Spouse Name: Robert Follick
Spouse's Age: 26
Spouse Birth Place: Canborough
Spouse Father Name: Jacob Follick
Spouse Mother Name : Rachel Follick
Marriage Date: 5 Jul 1874
Marriage Place: Elgin
Marriage County: Elgin

Robert and Mary can be found in the 1880 US Census in Pleasanton Twp., Manistee County Michigan. They had one son, Courtland/Cortland. [88]

1900 Michigan Census, Manistee County, Pleasanton Tp Roll 728 Book 1, Page 281
Robert H. Follick, b May 1848, 52, md 25 yrs 1 child, 1 child living, b Canada, imm 1877/97, Naturalized, in USA 23 yrs, farmer
Mary, b July 1852, Can [how can Mary be here in 1900 if her tombstone says she died in 1891?]
Cortland, son, b March 1877, b Canada, farm labourer

Robert remarried after the death of Mary to Louisa Keeler McGill. The marriage date given is 31 May 1901. [89]

1910 United States Federal Census Pleasanton, Manistee, Michigan
Household Members: Name Age
Robert Folic 62 born Canada English, head, parents born Canada English.
Immigrated 1879
Louise Folic 72 , wife
Cortland Folic 33, son

The family of Robert Follic (wife, son and grandsons) are buried in Pleasanton
Township Cemetery

Child of Robert Vollick and Mary Chambers is:
    75   i.   Cortland[11] Follick, born 22 Mar 1877 in Canada; died 1957 in
                   Manistee Michigan [90] .

    20. Jesse E.[10] Vollick (Jacob[9] Follick, Storm[8],) was born 13 Jan 1850 in
Canboro, Haldimand Co. Ontario [91] , and died 07 Feb 1921 in Dunnville, Haldimand
Co. Ontario [92] . He married **Eliza Winnie Sporbeck**, daughter of George Sperback
and Mary McFadden. She was born 16 Jun 1855 in N. Cayuga Tp. Haldimand Co
Ontario, and died 07 Aug 1926 in Dunnville, Haldimand Co. Ontario [93] .

Notes for Jesse E. Vollick:
1881 Census Dorchester North, Middlesex East, Ontario, Canada [94]
Jesse FOLLICK 29 German Ontario Occ:Toll Gate Keeper Religion: Regular Baptist
Eliza FOLLICK   27 German   Ontario   Religion:Regular Baptist
Alice FOLLICK   6 German   Ontario   Religion:Regular Baptist
Francis FOLLICK   4 German   Ontario   Religion:Regular Baptist

1901 Census of Canada Haldimand & Monck District Number: 67 Sub-District:
Canborough Sub-District Number: B-1 Family Number: 85 Page: 8

Jesse Follick 50 , born July 1851, German origin, head of house, farmer, Methodist,
born Ontario
Elza Follick 47
Frank Follick 23
Lincoln Follick 21
George J Follick 16
Cora Follick 14
Mary Follick 12
Richard Follick 6
Alice J Mariett 4/12 16 Mar 1901 grandaughter (must be Alice's daughter)

1911 Census District: Haldimand District Number: 75 Sub-District: Cayuga North
Sub-District Number: 6 Page: 7
Jessa Follick 1851
Eliza Follick 1865

Cora Follick 1887
Mary E Follick 1890
Richard A Follick 1895
Edmund Follick 1900 nephew
Henry Follick 1828 brother

Notes for Eliza Winnie Sporbeck:

Children of Jesse Vollick and Eliza Sporbeck are:

76	i.	Chancy[11] Follick, born 29 May 1873 in Haldimand Co. Ontario (Source: Chancey Follick 29 May 1873 Male Haldimand Jesse E Follick Eliza Sperback.); died 07 Aug 1874 in Canboro, Haldimand Co. Ontario;.
+ 77	ii.	Alma Alice Minerva Follick, born 07 May 1875 in Haldimand Co. Ontario;.
78	iii.	Francis (Frank) Edgar Follick, born 02 Jan 1877 in Middlesex Co. Ontario [95]; died 11 May 1911 in N. Cayuga Tp. Haldimand Co Ontario (Source: Ontario, Canada Deaths, 1869-1932 Haldimand 1911, Francis Edgar Follick, single, born Jan 2, 1877 Elgin Co. died 11 May 1911 Lot 23, Conc 1, N. Cayuga [96].);.
79	iv.	Lincoln Vollick, born 30 Sep 1879 in Ontario (Source: 1901 Census.).
+ 80	v.	Melissa Ann (Alice?) Follick, born 31 Mar 1882 in Middlesex Co. Ontario;.
81	vi.	George Jacob Follick, born 04 Jun 1884 in Middlesex Co. Ontario [97] died Aft. 18 May 1932 in Possibly Hamilton
82	vii.	Cora Vollick, born 31 Mar 1886 in Canboro, Haldimand Co, Ontario (Source: 1901 Census.); died 1970 in Dunnville Ontario.
+ 83	viii.	Mary Catherine Follick, born 30 Mar 1890 in N. Pelham, Welland Co. Ontario; died 06 Dec 1918 in Dunnville Ontario;.
+ 84	ix.	Richard Allen Follick, born 07 Aug 1894 in Welland Co. Ontario; died Aft. 07 Jul 1917;.

21. Isaac[10] Sperback (Sophia[9] Follick, Storm[8],) was born Abt. 1823 in Ontario, and died Aft. 1881. He married **Eliza Jane Tiller** Bef. 1858. She was born Abt. 1833 in Ontario, and died 15 Jan 1900 in Haldimand Co. Ontario (Source: Ontario, Canada Deaths, 1869-1932 Haldimand 1900, Eliza Ann Sporbeck, 62 years old, died Jan 15, 1900 born Canboro, living Main St, housewife, married died of LaGrippe had for 3 days. Baptist.).

Notes for Isaac Sperback:

1871 census Monck, Haldimand Page 17 Microfilm reel C-9918

1881 Census Place: Cayuga North, Haldimand, Ontario, Canada
Source: FHL Film 1375891 NAC C-13255 Dist 146 SubDist D Page 83 Family 386
Peter VOLLICK 34   German Ontario Occ: Farmer Religion: Episcopal Methodist

next door: Census Place: Cayuga North, Haldimand, Ontario, Canada
Source:FHL Film 1375891 NAC C-13255 Dist 146 SubDist D Page 83 Family 387
Isaac SPORBECK 58 German Ontario Occ: Farmer Religion: Episcopal Methodist
Eliza SPORBECK 48   German Ontario Religion:Episcopal Methodist
William SPORBECK 23 German Ontario Occ: Farmer Religion: Episcopal Methodist
Sophia SPORBECK 22 German Ontario Religion:Episcopal Methodist
John SPORBECK 19 German Ontario Religion:Episcopal Methodist Methodist
Ester SPORBECK 14 German Ontario Religion:Episcopal Methodist
Mary SPORBECK   F 11 German Ontario Religion:Episcopal Methodist

next door: Census Cayuga North, Haldimand, Ontario, Canada
Source: FHL Film 1375891 NAC C-13255 Dist 146 SubDist D Page 83 Family 388

Robert CAMPBELL   35 Scottish Ontario Occ: Labourer Religion: Episcopal
Methodist
Sophia CAMPBELL   30 Scottish   Ontario Religion: Episcopal Methodist
William CAMPBELL 5   Scottish   Ontario
Jenny CAMPBELL   3   Scottish   Ontario
Archie CAMPBELL   1   Scottish   Ontario

Children of Isaac Sperback and Eliza Tiller are:
+   85   i. James Nelson[11] Sperback, born 1856 in Canboro, Haldimand Co.
                  Ontario.
    86   ii. William Sperback, born Abt. 1858. He married Fannie Van Slack 03
                  Oct 1896 in Haldimand Co. Ontario; born Abt. 1877.
+   87   iii. Martha Jane Sperback, born Abt. 1859.
    88   iv. Sophia Sperback, born Abt. 1859.

89   v.   John W. Sperback, born Abt. 1862; died 20 Jan 1885 in Dunnville, Haldimand Co. Ontario (Source: Death Certificate, Laborer, died of pneumonia.).

90   vi. Ester Sperback, born Abt. 1867.

+ 91   vii. Mary Sperback, born Abt. 1870.

22. George[10] Sperback (Sophia[9] Follick, Storm[8],) was born Abt. 1825 in Canboro Tp Haldimand Co. Ontario, and died 20 November 1892 in Canboro, Haldimand Co. Ontario (Source: Death Certificate Canboro, Haldimand, #006174, George Sperback, male, 78 years old, farmer, Methodist, died of La Grippe. Informant John Sperback. Born Pelham.). He married **Mary McFadden**. She was born Abt. 1830 in Ireland or England or Wainfleet Tp, and died 18 Jun 1899 in Welland Co. Ontario.

Notes for George Sperback:
1861 Census Cayuga North Twp, Haldimand County
3 24 26 CRIBBINS Meriah UC W Methodist 40 F W
3 24 27 SPURBACK George laborer UC Episcopalian 29 M M
3 24 28 SPURBACK Maria IRE Episcopalian 29 F M
3 24 29 SPURBACK Eliza UC Episcopalian 8 F
3 24 30 SPURBACK John UC Episcopalian 4 M
3 24 31 SPURBACK Austin UC Episcopalian 3 M
3 24 32 SPURBACK Mary UC Episcopalian 1 F

1881 Census Place: Canborough, Monck, Ontario, Canada
FHL Film 1375890 NAC C-13254 Dist 144 SubDist F Div 1 Page 21 Family 115
George SPURBACK 56   Dutch OntarioOcc: Farmer Religion: E. Methodist
Mary SPURBACK 45 Irish Ireland   Religion: E. Methodist
John SPURBACK 23 Dutch OntarioOcc: Farmer   Religion: E. Methodist
Orston SPURBACK 21   Dutch OntarioOcc: Farmer Religion: E. Methodist
Sophia SPURBACK 18   Dutch Ontario   Religion: E. Methodist
Myria SPURBACK 15 Dutch Ontario   Religion: E. Methodist

Ontario, Canada Deaths, 1869-1932 > Welland > 1899
Mary Sporbeck d 18 June 1899, age 69, living 4th conc. a widow, born Wainfleet, died of "stricture". George Sporback was informant

Children of George Sperback and Mary McFadden are:
+ 92   i.   Eliza Winnie[11] Sporbeck, born 16 Jun 1855 in N. Cayuga Tp. Haldimand Co Ontario; died 07 Aug 1926 in Dunnville, Haldimand Co. Ontario.

93   ii. John Sperback, born Bet. 1850 - 1858; died Aft. 1901. He married Lydia Ann Lambert 16 Oct 1901 in Wentworth Co. Ontario; born Abt. 1850.

94   iii.   Austin Sperback, born 01 Apr 1858 in N. Cayuga Tp., Haldimand Co.
             Ontario; died 23 Mar 1924 in N. Cayuga Tp, Haldimand Co. Ontario
             (Source: Haldimand County Death Registrations, N. Cayuga Tp.
             Austin Spurbeck, married. 65 years 11 months 23 days old. Born
             April 1, 1858 N. Cayuga. Father George Spurbeck born North
             Pelham. Mother Mary McFadden born England. Lived 26 years
             current residence. Informant Manettie Spurbeck, wife, living Darling
             Road Buried Canboro March 25, 1924. Died of mitral incompetence,
             anemia and arterio sclerosis. Farmer.). He married Marietta
             (Manettie) Walker 10 Feb 1897 in Cayuga Tp Ontario; died Aft. Mar
             1924.
+   95   iv.   Sophia Catherine Sperback, born Abt. 1863 in North Cayuga,
             Haldimand Ontario.
+   96   v.   Maria Sperback, born Abt. 1865 in N. Cayuga, Haldimand Ontario.

27. Esther[10] Follick (Peter[9], Storm[8],) was born 24 Sep 1825 in Ontario, and
died 1918 in Indiana (Source: Death Cert states d.o.b. 24 Sept 1825.). She married
John Vetor 28 Feb 1854 in Canborough Ontario (Source:
<s7s7h8nb@coastainet.com>, *Correspondence of Linda Woods*, "Electronic."). He
was born 1811 in Germany, and died 28 May 1910 in IN.

Notes for John Vetor:

VETOR JOHN 76 M W GERM IN GRANT NATIONAL MILITARY HOME MARION
1900 Series: T623 Roll: 373 Page: 50 married, Destination Browne, MI, Nat.

1900 Fairmont, Grant, Indiana District 33
VETOR, Thomas, b Dec 1816 b Germ. imm 1830 Nat.
Ester, b Aug 1822, 11 children, 10 living, b Canada (Fr) imm 1865
Albert, b Dec 1853 b Camada imm 1865

GRANT FAIRMOUNT TWP 1910 Series: T624 Roll: 351 Page: 84
John Vetor, 92, b Germ, parents b Germ
Ester Vetor, 81, md 56 yrs, 12 children, 9 living, b Can Eng., father b PA, mother b
Germ,
Albert Vetor, 54, single, son , b Can Eng., house painter

Children of Esther Follick and John Vetor are:
    97   i.   Albert P.[11] Vetor, born 14 Dec 1854 in Ontario; died Aft. 1920.
    98   ii.   Sarah Vetor, born 15 Dec 1856 in Ontario.
+   99   iii. George Vetor, born 12 Sep 1858 in Ontario; died Bef. 1920.
    100   iv.   Martha Elizabeth Vetor, born 1860 in Ontario (Source: Don Haack
             (DVHaack@aol.com>, *Don Haack email*.); died 1959 in South Bend,
             St. Joseph Co. IL. She married Stephen L. Thorne 06 May 1882 in
             Madison Co. IL; died Aft. 1920.
+   101   v.   Frederick Storm Vetor, born 15 Dec 1861 in Ontario.

+	102	vi.	Henry Vetor, born 1864 in Ontario.
+	103	vii.	William A. Vetor, born 1866 in Indiana.
+	104	viii.	John Vetor, born 1868 in Indiana.
	105	ix.	Lavinia Vetor, born 20 May 1870 in Indiana.

28. Frederick[10] Follick (Peter[9], Storm[8],) was born Abt. 1834 in Canborough Tp. , Ontario, and died 15 Apr 1884 in Wainfleet, Welland Co. Ontario (Source: Welland County Death Registration, 018949-84 Wainfleet Tp. Frederick Follick, age 49, labourer, born Canboro Tp. Died of Inflamitory Rheumatism. His burial is found in the Canboro Cemetery as Fredrick Follick, age 49#005669. Canboro Tp Monck County: Frederick Follick died Apr. 15, 1884 age 49, of inflammation of the lungs. Born Canboro. Dr. Neff.). He married **Sarah Foster** Bef. 1865, daughter of Brock Foster and Jane Travis. She was born 24 Jul 1845 in Smithville, Caistor Tp, Ontario, and died 15 November 1927 in Wainfleet, Welland Co. Ontario (Source: Ontario, Canada Deaths, 1869-1932 Welland 1927, Sarah Follick, died Wainfleet, 82 years old, born 1845 in Smithxxxx. Father Brock Foster, born Nova Scotia. Mother Jane Travis born Smithville. Died November. 15, 1927, buried Canboro. Died of pneumonia and apoplexy.).

Notes for Frederick Follick:
1861 Cayuga Tp Haldimand Co. census

| 1 | 5 | 38 | FOLLICK | Fred | farmer | UC | Baptist | 32 M |

1881 Census Place: Wainfleet, Monck, Ontario, Canada
       Source: FHL Film 1375890 NAC C-13254 Dist 144 SubDist E Div 2 Page 18 Family 97
       SexMarr   Age   Origin Birthplace
Frederick FOLLICK 46 German Ontario Occ: Farmer Religion:Weslyan Methodist
Sarah FOLLICK 35 German Ontario Religion: Weslyan Methodist
Peter FOLLICK 16 German Ontario Occ: Farmer Religion: Weslyan Methodist
Burton FOLLICK 14   German Ontario Occ: Farmer Religion: Weslyan Methodist
Frederick FOLLICK 13 German Ontario Religion: Weslyan Methodist
Chandler FOLLICK 10 German Ontario Religion: Weslyan Methodist
Sarah FOLLICK 8 German Ontario Religion: Weslyan Methodist
Francis FOLLICK 6   German Ontario Religion: Weslyan Methodist
Solomon FOLLICK 4 German Ontario Religion: Weslyan Methodist
Queen FOLLICK 2 German Ontario Religion: Weslyan Methodist
Rosa FOLLICK <1 German Ontario Religion: Weslyan Methodist Born:Jan; 2/12

1891 Farmers Directory, Canboro Tp. Haldimand Co.

Folick, Andrew, Darling Rd., freeholder Clements Tract Lot 11
Folick, John, Darling Rd., freeholder Clements Tract Lot 11
Folick, Peter, Darling Rd., tenant, Clements Tract Lot 10
Folick, H.H., Darling Rd., tenant, Clements Tract Lot 10

*Folick, Frederick, Canboro, freeholder Conc 3 Lot 8
Folick, Jacob, Canboro, freeholder Conc 3 Lot 8
Vollick,Joel,Darling Road, freeholder Conc 3 Lot 8
Folick, J.W, Canboro, freeholder Conc 2 Lot 8

Death Registration: Wainfleet Tp. Frederick Follick, age 49, labourer, born Canboro Tp. Died of Inflamitory Rheumatism. His burial is found in the Canboro Cemetery as Fredrick Follick, age 49

Notes for Sarah Foster:
1901 census
2   24 Follick Fred M   Head S Dec 29 1867 33
3   24 Herrick Sarah F   Mother W Jul 24 1845 55
4   24 Follick Solomon M   Brother S November 21 1876 24

Children of Frederick Follick and Sarah Foster are:

106   i.   Peter Franklin[11] Follick, born 09 Jan 1865; died 27 Apr 1932 in Wainfleet, Welland Co. Ontario (Source: Ontario, Canada Deaths, 1869-1932 Welland 1932, Peter Frankllin Follick, residence Wainfleet, Welland Co. German origin, single, born Jan. 9, 1865, 67 years old, farmer, living 40 years in current residence, Father Frederick Follick, Mother Sarah Foster, Informant - Fred Follick of Wainfleet, brother. Died Apr. 27, 1932 of coronary thrombosis. Buried Wilson Wainfleet.).

107   ii. Burton Follick, born 06 Apr 1868 in Wainfleet Tp, Welland Co. Ontario; died 08 Mar 1926 in Wainfleet Tp, Welland Co. Ontario (Source: Death Registration # 085555 (MS 935 Reel 342) County of Welland, Division of Welland Surname: FOLLICK Full Given Name: Burton Place of Death: Welland County Hospital Sex: Male Racial Origin: Wainfleet Twp [sic] Trade: FarmerLength of Residence [at Welland County Hospital]: 5 weeks lived in Ontario: LifeFather: Frederick FOLLICK Birthplace of Father: North Cayuga Mother: Sarah Foster Birthplace of Mother: Smithville, Ontario Name of Informant: Peter FOLLICKAddress: Wainfleet R.R. #1Relation to Deceased: Brother Date of Burial: Mar.12, 1926 Undertaker: G.F.Sutherland of Welland Date of Death: Mar.8, 1926..).

108   iii. Frederick Follick, born 31 Dec 1867 (Source: 1901 Census.); died Aft. 27 Apr 1922.

109   iv. Chandler Follick, born Abt. 1871.

110   v.   Sarah Follick, born Abt. 1873.

111   vi. Francis Follick, born 16 May 1874; died 24 Dec 1900 in Canboro, Ontario.

112   vii. Solomon Follick, born 21 November 1876 (Source: 1901 Census.); died Aft. 1906.

113   viii.   Queen Victoria Follick, born 14 Jan 1879; died 13 Mar 1908 in

113   viii.   Queen Victoria Follick, born 14 Jan 1879; died 13 Mar 1908 in Canboro, Ontario.

+ 114   ix.   Rosa Ellen Follick, born 05 Mar 1881 in Welland Co. Ontario; died 26 Mar 1914 in Simcoe, Norfolk Co. Ontario.

115   x.   Andrew Follick, born 04 Apr 1884 in Welland Co. Ontario; died 04 Jul 1884 in Wainfleet Tp, Welland Co. Ontario (Source: Andrew Follick died 4 July 1884, Welland Co. 2 months old, laborer's child, born Wainfleet Tp, no cause of death noted. informant Sarah Follick of Marshville.).

32. Martha Elizabeth[10] Follick (Peter[9], Storm[8],) was born Abt. 16 Jul 1846 in Canboro, Haldimand Co. Ontario, and died 26 Feb 1916 in Niagara Falls, Welland Co. Ontario (Source: Martha Elizabeth McCormack, 69 years, 7 months, 10 days born Canboro. Died Feb 26, 1916 at 104 St Clair Ave, City [Niagara Falls]. Burial Port Colborne Ontario. WIdow. Father James [sic] Follick. no place of birth and no mother's name given. Informant: M. Morse & Son [Funeral Home] Died of pulmonary Tuberculosis had for 2 years, complicated by cardiac Failure.). She married **John McCormick** 13 Aug 1868 in Sherbrook, Haldimand Co. Ontario (Source: Name: Martha Follick Birth Place: Canboro Township Residence: Wainfleet Township Age: 20 Father Name: Peter Mother Name: Mary Estimated Birth Year: 1848 Spouse Name: John McCormick Spouse's Age: 26 Spouse Birth Place: Scotland Spouse Residence: Moulton Township Spouse Estimated Birth Year: 1842 Spouse Father Name: Angus Spouse Mother Name : An Benton Marriage Date: 13 Aug 1868 Marriage Place: Sherbrooke Marriage County: Haldimand Family History Library Microfilm: 1030057 .), son of Angus McCormick and Ann Benton. He was born 1842 in Scotland, and died Bef. Feb 1916.

Notes for Martha Elizabeth Follick:
1881 Census
John MCCORMIC M Male Scottish 47 Scotland Farmer E. Methodist
 Martha MCCORMIC M Female Scottish 35 Scotland E. Methodist
 Mary MCCORMIC Female Scottish 10 Ontario Going To School E. Methodist
 Harry MCCORMIC Male Scottish 2 Ontario E. Methodist
 Emanuel MCCORMIC Male Scottish <1 Born: November; 5/12 November
Ontario E. Methodist
Source Information: Census Place Humberstone, Welland, Ontario
 Family History Library Film 1375889 NA Film Number C-13253 District 142
 Sub-district A Division 1 Page Number 95 Household Number 382

Source Information: 1901 Census of Canada
Subdistrict: Canborough, HALDIMAND & MONCK, ONTARIO
District Number: 67 Subdistrict Number: b-2 Archives Microfilm: T-6470

6 8 58 Robins Hezekiah M Head M Aug 29 1825, 75
6 9 58 Robins Martha F Wife M Jan 22 1840, 61
6 10 58 Follick Peter M Domestic S Sep 5 1862, 38

6 2 56 Follick John K M Head M Aug 31 1849 51
6 3 56 Follick Maria F Wife M Jun 19 1860 40
6 4 56 Follick Gertie F Daughter S Sep 19 1884 16
6 5 56 Follick Curtis M Son S Feb 13 1892 9
6 6 57 Follick Andrew M Head M Dec 18 1842 58
6 7 57 Follick Nancy J F Wife M Jul 15 1870 30

6 17 61 Follick Henry M Head S May 21 1828 72

1911 Canada Census Record District: Haldimand District Number: 75 Sub-District: Canboro Sub-District Number: 1 Census Year: 1911 Page: 5
Martha Robins head born May 1836, widow, 74
Peter Follick domestic b June 1861
Emma Cline domestic b Apr 1890

nearby is Mahlon S Follick, domestic, born Aug 1842, Baptist. Widowed Age: 68 Birth Date: August 1842 Birthplace: Ontario Family Number: 59 Relation to Head of House: Domestic Tribal: German

Child of Martha Follick and John McCormick is:
   116   i.   Mary Ann[11] McCormick, born Abt. 1872; died 12 May 1933 in
              Welland County Ontario.

   34. John K.[10] Follick (Peter[9], Storm[8],) was born 31 Aug 1849 in Canboro, Haldimand Co. Ontario, and died 01 November 1907 in Canboro Tp, Haldimand Co. Ontario (Source: Haldimand County Death Registrations, John K Follick died November. 1, 1907, 59 years old. Farmer living Darling Road, Canboro Tp, married. born Canboro Tp, died of dilation of heart had for one month.). He married **(1) Maria Foster** 06 Mar 1884 in Canborough Tp. Haldimand Co. Ontario (Source: Name: John R. Folick Spouse Name: Maria Foster Marriage Date: 6 Mar 1884 Marriage Place: Canborough Township Registration Number: 003944 Archives of Ontario Microfilm: 46 .). She was born 19 Jun 1860, and died Bef. 1892. He married **(2) Maria Sporbeck** Aft. 1891.

Notes for John K. Follick:
1881 Census Place: Canborough, Monck, Ontario, Canada
FHL Film 1375890 NAC C-13254 Dist 144 SubDist F Div 2 Page 4 Family 21
John FOLICK 32 German Ontario Occ:Farmer Religion: E. Methodist
Andrew FOLICK 38 German Ontario Occ: Farmer Religion: E. Methodist
Ellen FOLICK 28 German Ontario Religion: E. Methodist
Ellen FOLICK widow, 70 Irish Ireland Religion: E. Methodist

1891 Farmers Directory, Canboro Tp. Haldimand Co.
Folick, Andrew, Darling Rd., freeholder Clements Tract Lot 11
*Folick, John, Darling Rd., freeholder Clements Tract Lot 11

Folick, Peter, Darling Rd., tenant, Clements Tract Lot 10
Folick, H.H., Darling Rd., tenant, Clements Tract Lot 10

Folick, Frederick, Canboro, freeholder Conc 3 Lot 8
Folick, Jacob, Canboro, freeholder Conc 3 Lot 8
Vollick,Joel,Darling Road, freeholder Conc 3 Lot 8
Folick, J.W, Canboro, freeholder Conc 2 Lot 8

1901 census District: Ontario HALDIMAND & MONCK (#67) Subdistrict:
Canborough b-1 Page 7 Details: Schedule 1 Microfilm T-6470

13 77 Follick John W M Head M Feb 26 1862 38
14 77 Follick Callie E F Wife M Mar 17 1868 32
15 77 Follick Eva May F Daughter S Mar 18 1886 14
16 77 Follick Violet A F Daughter S Apr 9 1890 10
17 77 Follick Nathen E M Son S Jun 2 1891 9
18 77 Follick Richard A M Son S Mar 18 1893 7
19 77 Follick Edna F Daughter S November 6 1898 1
20 77 Follick Edmond M Son S November 6 1898 1
21 77 Follick John S M Lodger W Oct 8 1850 50

1901 District: Ontario HALDIMAND & MONCK (#67) Subdistrict: Canborough b-2
Page 6 Details: Schedule 1 Microfilm T-6470

2 56 Follick John K M Head M Aug 31 1849 51
3 56 Follick Maria F Wife M Jun 19 1860 40
4 56 Follick Gertie F Daughter S Sep 19 1884 16
5 56 Follick Curtis M Son S Feb 13 1892 9
6 57 Follick Andrew M Head M Dec 18 1842 58
7 57 Follick Nancy J F Wife M Jul 15 1870 30

next door is brother Andrew

Children of John Follick and Maria Foster are:
    117   i. Gertie May[11] Follick, born 19 Sep 1884 in Haldimand Co. Ontario.
    118   ii. Edmund Follick, born 17 Aug 1897 in Niagara Falls, Welland Co. Ontario.

Child of John Follick and Maria Sporbeck is:
    119   i. Curtis[11] Follick, born 13 Feb 1892 in Haldimand Co. Ontario (Source: Curtis Follick 13 Feb 1892 Male Haldimand John K Follick Mariah Sperback.); died 05 Jul 1937 in Dunnville, Ontario. [98]

35. Sophia Catherine[10] Follick (Peter[9], Storm[8],) was born 04 Mar 1851 in Haldimand Co. Ontario, and died 06 Mar 1927 in Glencor, Middlesex Co. Ontario (Source: Ontario, Canada Deaths, 1869-1932 Middlesex 1927, Sophia Catharine

Campbell, Dutch and English origin, died at Glencoe. Married, 76 years 2 days old, bornMarch 4, Haldimand Co. , housewife. Lived 4 mos at place of residence. Father Peter Follick born Haldimand, Mother Ellen Crane. Informant Archie Campbell of Newbury, son. Buried March 8, 1927 Okland. Died March 6th of pleural pneumonia.). She married **Robert Campbell** 04 Jun 1874 in Canborough Ontario (Source: *Vital Statistics*, M/F 114 #3878 courtesy of Corlene Taylor, Robert Campbell, 29, res. N. Cayuga, farmer b Ont. s/o Archibald & Jane m 4 June 1874 Sophia Follick 23 d/o Peter & Ellen. Wit Ellen Follick, Canboro, John M Teetor N. Cauyga.), son of Archibald Campbell and Jane. He was born Abt. 1845 in N. Cayuga Tp. Ontario.

Notes for Sophia Catherine Follick:
Robert Campbell, 29, res. N. Cayuga, farmer, b. Ontario s/o Archibald and Jane md. 4 June 1874 Sophia Follick, 23, d/o Peter & Ellen. Witnesses Ellen Follick, Canboro and John M. Teeter, N. Cayuga. He Presbyterian, she Methodist.

Living next door to Sophia and Robert in 1881 is
Census Place: Cayuga North, Haldimand, Ontario, Canada FHL Film 1375891 NAC C-13255 Dist 146 SubDist D Page 83 Family 387
Isaac SPORBECK 58 German Ontario Occ: Farmer Religion: Episcopal Methodist
Eliza SPORBECK 48 German Ontario Religion: Episcopal Methodist
William SPORBECK 23 German Ontario Occ: Farmer Religion: Episcopal Methodist
Sophia SPORBECK 22 German Ontario Religion: Episcopal Methodist
John SPORBECK 19 German, farmer, Ontario Religion: Episcopal Methodist
Ester SPORBECK 14 German Ontario Religion: Episcopal Methodist
Mary SPORBECK 11 German Ontario Religion: Episcopal Methodist

Notes for Robert Campbell:
1881 Census Place: Cayuga North, Haldimand, Ontario, Canada
FHL Film 1375891 NAC C-13255 Dist 146 SubDist D Page 83 Family 388
Robert CAMPBELL 35 Scottish Ontario Occ: Labourer Religion: Episcopal Methodist
Sophia CAMPBELL 30 Scottish Ontario Religion: Episcopal Methodist
William CAMPBELL 5 Scottish Ontario Religion: Episcopal Methodist
Jenny CAMPBELL   3 Scottish Ontario Religion: Episcopal Methodist
Archie CAMPBELL   1 Scottish Ontario Religion: Episcopal Methodist

Children of Sophia Follick and Robert Campbell are:
- 120   i.   William John[11] Campbell, born 07 Aug 1876 in Haldimand Co. Ontario.
- 121   ii.   Jenny Campbell, born 10 Mar 1878 in Haldimand Co. Ontario.
- 122   iii.   Archie Campbell, born Abt. 1880 in Haldimand County Ontario. He married Lottie McKim 29 Dec 1917 in Kent Co. Ontario.
- 123   iv.   George Campbell, born Abt. 1883. He married Nettie P. Ball 23 Mar 1910 in Kent Co. Ontario; born Abt. 1884.

124   v.   Ruthey Edith Campbell, born Abt. 1893 in Romney Ontario. She married Vincent Watterworth 06 May 1914 in Middlesex County Ontario.

36. Ellen (Nellie)[10] Follick (Peter[9], Storm[8],) was born Oct 1852 in Dunnville, Haldimand Co. Ontario, and died 28 Feb 1926 in Tillbury East, Kent Co. Ontario (Source: Ontario, Canada Deaths, 1869-1932 Kent 1926, Ellen Gifford, 73 years 4 mos old born Dunnville, Haldimand Co. in 1852. Irish-Dutch origin. Married housewife, lived current residence 30 years. Father Mr. Follic, born Haldimand Co. Mother Ellen Crane, born Ireland. Informant. G. A. Gifford of RR 4, Merlin, her husband. Died of Septicimea Feb 28, 1926.). She married **George Avery Gifford** 13 Oct 1881 in Dunnville, Haldimand Co. Ontario (Source: 003796-81 (Haldimand Co) George GIFFORD, 30, Farmer, Dunnville, same, s/o Maxwell & Maria GIFFORD married Nellie FOLLICK, 29, Canboro, same d/o Peter & Ellen FOLLICK, witn: John FOLLICK & Mary FOSTER both of Canboro, 13 October 1881 at Dunnville.), son of Maxwell Gifford and Maria. He was born Abt. 1851.

Notes for Ellen (Nellie) Follick:
Name: Nellie Follick
Birth Place: Carrboro
Age: 29
Father Name: Peter Follick
Mother Name: Ellen Follick
Estimated Birth Year: abt 1852
Spouse Name: George Gifford
Spouse's Age: 30
Spouse Birth Place: Dunn
Spouse Father Name: Maxwell Gifford
Spouse Mother Name : Maria Gifford
Marriage Date: 13 Oct 1881
Marriage Place: Haldimand
Marriage County: Haldimand

Children of Ellen Follick and George Gifford are:
    125   i.   Robert[11] Gifford, born 04 Oct 1882 in Haldimand Co. Ontario.
    126   ii.   Nellie May Gifford, born Abt. 1887 in Tilbury East Twp. She married Thomas Martin Johnson 06 November 1907 in Kent Co. Ontario; born in Tilbury East Twp
    127   iii.   Donald Gifford, born 03 Mar 1893 in Kent Co. Ontario.

37. George Alexander[10] Follick (Matthias[9], Storm[8],) was born 10 Oct 1832 in Canboro, Haldimand Co. Ontario, and died 23 Feb 1911 in Montpelier, Bear Lake County Idaho. He married **Nancy Parker** 31 Dec 1857 in Haldimand Co. Ontario (Source: Haldimand Co. Marriages & Burials, 1851-65, 31 Dec 1857. George A Folick, 21 - Nancy Parker, 18 Rev SW Folyer.), daughter of Abel Parker and Isabella

Marshall. She was born 08 Sep 1838 in Canboro, Haldimand Co. Ontario, and died 19 May 1908 in Montpelier, Bear Lake County Idaho.

Notes for George Alexander Follick:
Haldimand Co. Marriages 1851-1865: 31 Dec. 1857 - George A. Follick, 21 and Nancy Parker, 18. Rev. SW Folyer

#1297 Bargain and Sale

Mary Maria Vollick
John Stome?? Vollick and wife
Isaac Hartman Vollick
Peter Mathias Vollick
Joseph William Vollick
Heirs of the late George Vollick deceased to Joel Vollick Lot 3, 55 acres
Clement Tract for $500

1860 Census Series: M653 Roll: 336   Page: 21   Plattville Township 1860 Census
Mills County, Iowa
Follick, George, 27 / m / blacksmith / Canada
Follick, Nancy, 21 / f / Canada
Follick, Isabel, 1 / f / IA

1870 Census UTAH CEDAR FORT   Series: M593   Roll: 1612   Page: 199
Follick, George 36 b Can
Nancy 31 b Can
Isabel 11 b Iowa
David 9 b Can (scribbled on)
Claude 4 b Can (scribbled on)
James 9 mos b Utah

1900 Census Dingle, Bear Lake, Idaho

Follick, George b Oct 1832 b Canada, immigrated 1857, blacksmith
Nancy b Sept 1838 10 children, 6 living, b Canada
Margaret A. daughter b June 1874 b Utah
Mary, grand-daughter b Sept 1896 b Utah

WW1 Draft Registrations
Follick, Charles Loraine   b 14 Jan 1889 W Montpelier ID   Bear Lake   ID
Follick, David Romaine   b   20 Oct 1886 W Montpelier ID   Bear Lake   ID
Follick, George Reuel   b 19 Jul 1899 W   Bear Lake   ID

Pioneers and Prominent Men of Utah, Genealogies and Biographies, F. Privates

FOLLICK, GEORGE ALEXANDER (son of Mathias Follick and Rachel McLaughlln of Canboro, Canada). Born Oct. 12, 1831, Canboro, Canada. Came to Utah June, 1868, Capt. Taylor company. Married Nancy Parker April 15, 1857, Canboro, Canada (daughter of Abel Parker and Isabel Marshall of Youngstown, N. Y.pioneers June, 1863), who was born Sept. 8, 1838. Their children: Isabel, m. F. M. Dayton; David, m. Marlan Bridges: Mattie, died in childhood; Claude, m. Mary Blaser; James and George, d. children; Mary Jane. m. William F. Dayton: Margaret Ann, m. Roy George; Abel Mathias, d. child: Martha, m. John R. George. Blacksmith, carpenter and miner. Died Feb. 25, 1911, Montpelier, Idaho.

Notes for Nancy Parker:
Bridgewater or Owens Cemetery FOLLICK, Nancy Died: 3/23/1909, Age: 75 yrs. Relative: George Follick, Stewart Records

Children of George Follick and Nancy Parker are:
- 128   i.   Isabel[11] Follick, born 20 Oct 1858 in Bethlehem, Mills County Indiana; died 03 Jan 1947 in Montpelier, Bear Lake County, Idaho. She married Francis M. Dayton.
- + 129   ii.   David Follick, born 30 Dec 1860 in Egypt, Fremont County Indiana; died 02 Jul 1921 in Montpelier, Bear Lake County Idaho.
- 130   iii. Mattie Follick, born 20 Jun 1863 in Denver, Jefferson County CO; died 18 Jul 1865.
- 131   iv.   Claude Follick, born 13 Jun 1866 in Denver, Jefferson County CO; died 06 Aug 1906 in Montpelier, Bear Lake County Idaho. He married Mary Blaser.
- 132   v.   James Warren Follick, born 27 Oct 1869 in Cedar Fort, Utah County UT; died 05 Jan 1873.
- 133   vi.   George Alexander Follick, born 09 November 1871 in Cedar Fort, Utah County UT; died 05 Jan 1873.
- 134   vii. Margaret Ann Follick, born 07 Jan 1874 in Tooele, Tooele County UT; died 11 Mar 1938 in Ogden, Weber Co. Utah. She married Roy George.
- 135   viii. Mary Jane Follick, born 07 Jan 1874 in Tooele, Tooele County UT; died 16 Jul 1926 in Salt Lake City, Utah. She married William F. Dayton.
- 136   ix.   Abel Mathias Follick, born 19 Aug 1877 in Tooele, Tooele County UT; died 06 Oct 1889.
- 137   x.   Martha Follick, born 18 May 1880 in Montpelier, Bear Lake County ID; died 21 November 1964 in Rupert Idaho. She married John R. George.

38. Catherine[10] Follick (Matthias[9], Storm[8],) was born 17 Feb 1833 in Canboro, Haldimand Co. Ontario, and died 11 May 1874. She married **John Motley**. He was born 31 Aug 1831.

Children of Catherine Follick and John Motley are:

138   i.   George[11] Motley, born Abt. 1871 in Cayuga, Gosfield South, Essex Co. Ontario. He married Esther Ann Marrot 17 Jan 1900 in Ruthven, Essex Co. Ontario (Source: #005100-00 (Essex Co): George MOTLEY, 29, farmer, Cayuga, Gosfield South, s/o John MOTLEY & Catherine VOLLICK, married Esther Ann MARRETT, 25, Gosfield S., same, d/o James MERRITT & Alvineda? WIGLE, 17 Jan 1900 at Ruthven.).

139   ii.   Bessie Motley, born in St. Catharines Ontario. She married William Fleming 26 Mar 1883 in Essex County Ontario; born in Durham England.

40. Rachel[10] Follick (Matthias[9], Storm[8],) was born 1836, and died 31 May 1891. She married **James W. Warren**. He was born Abt. 1842.

Notes for James W. Warren:

1871 Census District MONCK (018) Sub-district Gainsborough (E)Division 1 Page 9 Microfilm reel C-9918

1881   Census Place: Canborough, Monck, Ontario, Canada FHL Film 1375890 NAC C-13254 Dist 144 SubDist F Div 2 Page 10 Family 52
James WARREN 39   English England Occ: Farmer Religion: Baptist
Rachel WARREN 41 German Ontario Religion: Baptist
Agness A. WARREN 17 English Ontario Religion: Baptist
James H. WARREN   15 English Ontario Religion: Baptist
Margaret E. WARREN 11 English Ontario Religion: Baptist
Eugene E. WARREN 9 English Ontario Religion: Baptist
John S. WARREN 7 English Ontario Religion: Baptist
William W. WARREN 4 English Ontario Religion: Baptist
Arthur E. WARREN 1 English Ontario Religion Baptist

Children of Rachel Follick and James Warren are:
140   i.   Agnes A.[11] Warren, born 09 Mar 1864 (Source: IGI 1993).
141   ii. James H. Warren, born Abt. 1866.
142   iii. Margaret Emily Warren, born 28 Sep 1869 in Haldimand Co. Ontario.
+ 143 iv. Eugene Edgar Warren, born 19 Jul 1872 in Canboro, Ontario; died 1949.
144   v. John S. Warren, born 17 Aug 1874 (Source: IGI 1993).
145   vi. William W. Warren, born 24 Dec 1877 (Source: IGI 1993).

146 vii. Arthur E. Warren, born Abt. 1880.

41. Joel[10] **Follick** (Matthias[9], Storm[8],) was born 22 Jun 1838 in Canboro, Haldimand Co. Ontario, and died 25 Feb 1899 in Lincoln Co. Ontario (Source: Ontario, Canada Deaths, 1869-1932 Lincoln 1899, Joel Vollick, died Feb 25, 1899, 61 years old, residence part of lot 8, conc. 9, farmer born Canboro Tp, died of cancer that he had for 8 months, Baptist.). He married **Susanna White** 03 Jan 1871 (Source: Vital Stats, Joel Vollick age 27 born Canboro, son of Matthias & Gitta to Susannah White age 21 on Jan 3, 1871.). She was born Abt. 1850, and died 09 Feb 1903 in Haldimand Co. Ontario (Source: Ontario, Canada Deaths, 1869-1932 Haldimand 1903, Death Cert: Susanna VOLLICK, Feb. 9, 1902 age 52 years. Lived on Main Street. Widow. Consumption of lungs. Baptist.).

1881 Census Place: Canborough, Monck, Ontario, Canada
FHL Film 1375890 NAC C-13254 Dist 144 SubDist F Div 1 Page 25 Family 132
Joel VOLICK   39   Dutch OntarioOcc: Carpenter   Religion: Baptist
Susannah VOLICK 31   Dutch Ontario   Religion: E. Methodist
Margret E. VOLICK   3   Dutch Ontario   Religion: E. Methodist

1891 Farmers Directory, Canboro Tp. Haldimand Co.
Folick, Andrew, Darling Rd., freeholder Clements Tract Lot 11
Folick, John, Darling Rd., freeholder Clements Tract Lot 11
Folick, Peter, Darling Rd., tenant, Clements Tract Lot 10
Folick, H.H., Darling Rd., tenant, Clements Tract Lot 10
Folick, Frederick, Canboro, freeholder Conc 3 Lot 8
Folick, Jacob, Canboro, freeholder Conc 3 Lot 8
*Vollick,Joel,Darling Road, freeholder Conc 3 Lot 8
Folick, J.W, Canboro, freeholder Conc 2 Lot 8

Child of Joel Follick and Susanna White is:
   147   i. Margaret Ellen[11] Vollick, born 08 May 1878 in Canboro, Haldimand Co. Ontario (Source: Birth registration); died 09 Sep 1892 in Canboro, Haldimand Co. Ontario (Source: *Death Registration*, Vital Stats 006133-92, Margaret Ellen Vollick died 9 Sept 1892 age 14 from Canboro; always sick, do not know why; Methodist. Father James Oscar Vollick.).

42. Cynthia E.[10] **Follick** (Matthias[9], Storm[8],) was born 04 Jul 1840 in Canboro, Haldimand Co. Ontario, and died 20 Jul 1916 in Pt. Colborne, Ontario [99]She married **Jacob Root** 13 Feb 1877 in Caledonia, Ontario [100] son of John Root and Hannah. He was born 12 Jun 1839 in Sherbrook, and died 26 Feb 1894 in Pt. Colborne, Ontario and is buried Overholt Cemetery, Pt. Colborne, Ontario.

1871 Census District MONCK (018)Sub-district Moulton & Sherbrook (A)Division 1 Page 4Microfilm reel C-9918

ROOT, JACOB Age: 30 Birthplace ONTARIO Religion Baptist Origin DUTCH Occupation Farmer (F)

Marriage: Name: Jacob Root Birth Place: Sherbrooke Age: 36 Father Name: John Root Mother Name: Hannah Root Spouse Name: Cinthia Vollick Spouse's Age: 35 Spouse Birth Place: Carrboro Spouse Father Name: Mathew Vollick Spouse Mother Name : Guitty Vollick Marriage Date: 13 Feb 1877 Marriage Place: Haldimand Marriage County: Haldimand

1881   Census Place: Sherbrooke, Monck, Ontario, Canada
FHL Film 1375890 NAC C-13254 Dist 144 SubDist D Page 18 Family 86

Jacob ROOT	40	English, Ontario	Occ: Farmer	Religion:	Baptist
Cynthia ROOT	39	Scottish	Ontario Religion:	I E Methodist	
Hattie ROOT	12	English	Ontario Religion:	I E Methodist	
James A. ROOT	10	English	Ontarip Religion:	I E Methodist	
George A. ROOT	3	English	Ontario Religion:	I E Methodist	

1901 Census of Canada District: Ontario WELLAND (#123) Subdistrict: Humberstone F-3 Page 9 Details: Schedule 1 Microfilm T-6503
Root Cynthia F Head W Jul 4 1840 60
Root George A. M   Son S November 24 1877 23
Root John M. M   Son S Apr 1 1882 19

Children of Cynthia Follick and Jacob Root are:
   148   i.   Hattie[11] Root, born Abt. 1869.
   149   ii.   James A. Root, born Abt. 1871.
   150   iii.   George Arthur Root, born 24 Dec 1877 in Haldimand Co. Ontario [101]d
                  ied 1939. He married Mildred Putman 18 Sep 1918 in Haldimand
                  Co. Ontario; born Abt. 1879 in Welland Co. Ontario.
   151   iv.   John Matthias Root, born 01 Apr 1882 in Haldimand Co. Ontario [102]
                  died 1953 in Pt. Colborne, Ontario, and is buried in Overholt
                  Cemetery. He married Ethel Blanche Shisler.

      43. Jesse Malon (Macon or Macow) Edwin[10] Follick (Matthias[9], Storm[8],) was born 08 November 1842 in Canboro, Haldimand Co. Ontario, and died 05 Feb 1918 in Canboro, Haldimand Co. Ontario [103] He married **(1) Eliza Rew?**. She was born 10 Jun 1853 in Ontario, and died Aft. 1921. He married **(2) Isabella Jones** Bef. 1872. She died Bef. 1911.

Notes for Jesse Malon (Macon or Macow) Edwin Follick:
1871 census S. Cayuga Tp. Haldimand Co. George Follick along with Ellen b. 1816 Ire., Jacob b. 1802, Jacob b. 1843, Jesse b. 1844, Mary b. 1826 and Matthias b. 1813

1881 Census Place:Dorchester North, Middlesex East, Ontario, Canada FHL Film 1375904 NAC C-13268 Dist 167 SubDist B Div 2 Page 13 Family 64

Jesse FOLLICK, 29   German, Ontario Occ:Toll Gate Keeper Religion:RegularBaptist
Eliza FOLLICK, 27   German   Ontario   Religion: Regular Baptist
Alice FOLLICK, 6   German   Ontario   Religion: Regular Baptist
Francis FOLLICK, 4   German   Ontario   Religion: Regular Baptist

<u>1891 Farmers Directory, Canboro Tp. Haldimand Co.</u>
Folick, Andrew, Darling Rd., freeholder Clements Tract Lot 11
Folick, John, Darling Rd., freeholder Clements Tract Lot 11
Folick, Peter, Darling Rd., tenant, Clements Tract Lot 10
Folick, H.H., Darling Rd., tenant, Clements Tract Lot 10
Folick, Frederick, Canboro, freeholder Conc 3 Lot 8
Folick, Jacob, Canboro, freeholder Conc 3 Lot 8
Vollick,Joel,Darling Road, freeholder Conc 3 Lot 8
*Folick, J.W, Canboro, freeholder Conc 2 Lot 8

<u>1901 Census District: Ontario HALDIMAND & MONCK (#67) Subdistrict:Canborough</u>
<u>b-1 Page 1</u> Details: Schedule 1 Microfilm T-6470
Warren James M   Head M Mar 30 1867 34
Warren Jesse H. F   Wife M Jul 31 1871 29
Warren Belle F   Daughter S November 6 1893 7
Warren Pearl E F   Daughter S Jun 14 1896 4
Warren Robert M   Son S November 19 1897 3
Warren Ruby J F   Daughter S Apr 23 1900 11/12
Follick Malon J M   Lodger W Aug 8 1842 58

<u>1911 Census District: Haldimand District Number: 75 Sub-District: Canboro Sub-</u>
<u>District Number: 1 Page: 5</u>
James H Morren 1866
Bell G Morren 1891
Robert Morren 1897
Pearl E Morren 1894
Roby J Morren 1900
Charles Morren 1902
Gordon Morren 1903
Agnes A Morren 1864
Mahlon J Follick Widowed, Age: 68 Birth Date: August 1842 Birthplace: Ontario

Children of Jesse Follick and Isabella Jones are:
+   152   i.   Cynthia (Isabelle? Catharine?)[11] Vollick, born 05 May 1872 in
                  Walsingham?; died Aft. 1901 in Haldimand Co. Ontario?.
    153   ii.   Mathias Elmore Vollick, born 1872 in Essex Co. Ontario; died 1935
                  in Stratford, Ontario. He married Sarah Jessie Longfoot 04 Sep 1912
                  in Stratford, Perth Co. Ontario; born in Stratford, Perth Co. Ontario.

45. Henry Harvey[10] Vollick (Matthias[9] Follick, Storm[8],) was born 26 Dec 1849
in Canboro, Haldimand Co. Ontario, and died 28 Jun 1899 in Tillbury, Kent Co.

Ontario [104]. He married **Alice Augusta Saunders** 18 November 1891 in Dunnville Ontario, daughter of Charles Saunders and Mary Cutler. She was born Abt. 1869 in Canboro, Haldimand Co. Ontario and died in Niagara Falls, New York.

1881 Census Place: Canborough, Monck, Ontario, Canada
FHL Film 1375890 NAC C-13254 Dist 144 SubDist F Div 2 Page 13 Family 67
Gittee VOLLICK, widow, 62 Irish   Ontario Occ: Farmer Religion: Baptist
Henry H. VOLLICK 31, German., Ontario Occ:Farmer Religion: Baptist
Cynthia I. VOLLICK   7 German., Ontario Religion:Baptist

Marriage: Name: Alice A Saunders Birth Place: Carrboro Age: 22 Father Name: Charles Saunders Mother Name: Mary Saunders Spouse Name: Henry H Vollick Spouse's Age: 40 Spouse Birth Place: Carrboro Spouse Father Name: Matthias Vollick Spouse Mother Name : Gettie Vollick Marriage Date: 18 November 1891 Marriage Place: Haldimand Marriage County: Haldimand

1891 Farmers Directory, Canboro Tp. Haldimand Co.
Folick, Andrew, Darling Rd., freeholder Clements Tract Lot 11
Folick, John, Darling Rd., freeholder Clements Tract Lot 11
Folick, Peter, Darling Rd., tenant, Clements Tract Lot 10
*Folick, H.H., Darling Rd., tenant, Clements Tract Lot 10

Folick, Frederick, Canboro, freeholder Conc 3 Lot 8
Folick, Jacob, Canboro, freeholder Conc 3 Lot 8
Vollick,Joel,Darling Road, freeholder Conc 3 Lot 8
Folick, J.W, Canboro, freeholder Conc 2 Lot 8

Notes for Alice Augusta Saunders:
Taken from the Lane Funeral Home of Niagara Falls, New York regarding their file on Alice (Saunders),wife of Henry Harvey Vollick, and subsequently William Hayes.

Their records state that she was born in Dunville [sic] Ontario to William Saunders [sic]. Her mother's name is not recorded [her mother was Mary Catherine Cutler]. Alice was the wife of the late WilliamHayes. They are both buried in Oakwood Cemetery, Niagara Falls New York.

Alice was survived by her two children, Mrs. Robert Irwin of Niagara Falls Ontario, & Robert Vollick of Niagara Falls, New York. Also by grandchildren and great grandchildren.

New York NIAGARA CAMBRIA 1920 Series: T625 Roll: 1240   Page: 4
VOLLICK ALICE A, servant, 49 yrs old, born Canada, a widow, unknown year of immigration

Children of Henry Vollick and Alice Saunders are:

+ 154   i.   Mary Alice[11] Vollick, born 18 November 1892 in Romney Tp. Kent Co. Ontario; died 30 Dec 1974.

155   ii.   Joseph Stanley Vollick, born 23 November 1897 in Dunnville, Essex Co. Ontario [105] died 09 Apr 1917 in Vimy, Pas de Calais, France [106]

156   iii. Robert Vollick, born 29 Jun 1900 died Jan 1965 in Niagara Falls, New York. [107] He married Eleanor Larabee.

46. John Storm (Storm?)[10] Follick (George[9], Storm[8],) was born 08 Oct 1850 in Canboro, Haldimand Co, Ontario, and died 04 Jun 1928 in Dunnville, Haldimand Co. Ontario (Source: Ontario, Canada Deaths, 1869-1932 Haldimand 1928, John Storms [sic] Follick, 67 years old, born Ontario in 1860, father George Follick, mother Maria. Farmer, widower. Informant Henry Edwin Follick of Dunnville, cousin. Died in the War Memorial Hospital on June 4, of Chronic myocardial degeneration.). He married **Margaret Martha McLaughlin** 08 Oct 1879 in Dunnville, Haldimand Co. Ontario (Source: 003560-1880 (Haldimand Co.) John S. FOLLICK, 25, Farmer, Canboro, same, s/o Geo & Maria, married Margaret McLAUGHLIN, 29, Canboro, Canboro, d/o Jas & Catharine, witn: Harriett & Emma WILSON both of Dunnville, 8 Oct 1879 at Dunnville.), daughter of James McLaughlin and Catharine. She was born Abt. 1850 in Canboro, Haldimand Co, Ontario, and died Bef. 1901.

Notes for John Storm (Storm?) Follick:
1901 see John William Follick and family in Subdistrict: Canborough, HALDIMAND & MONCK, ONTARIO District Number: 67 Subdistrict Number: b-1 Archives Microfilm: T-6470 He is a lodger and a widower

1916 9-03 (Welland Co): James SMITH, 37, widower, railroader, Simcoe Ont., Niagara Falls South, s/o David SMITH & Mary Ann MAYO, married Ella FOLLICK, 24, Canboro, Niagara Falls South, d/o Storm FOLLICK & unknown, witn: George McCLELLAN & Dora REDPATH, both of Niagara Falls South, 15 November 1903 at Niagara Falls South

Children of John Follick and Margaret McLaughlin are:

157   i.   Edna Malvina[11] Follick, born 1880 in Haldimand Co. Ontario.

158   ii.   Minnie Follick, born Abt. 1890 in Canboro Township, Haldimand Co. Ontario. She married George William House 13 Jul 1914 in Haldimand Co. Ontario; born Abt. 1874 in Moulton Tp Ontario.

+ 159   iii. possibly Ellen Melinda Follick, born 18 Dec 1878 in Ontario.

FAMILY RECORD.

DEATHS.	DEATHS.
Parents	died at *[illegible]*
Jacob Follick, Senr.	July 23rd 1887 buried at Canton 24th
Rachel Follick	July 26th 1865

FAMILY RECORD.

BIRTHS.	BIRTHS.
Jacob Follick Senr. his funeral text was Psalms XVII — 15 verse by Rev. Pugsly Baptist minister	October — 1800
Elizabeth Lossing was born August — 1797 Elizabeth Lossing died August 8th 1883	

Jacob Follick
1800-1897
&
Rachel Smith

Eva May Follick
   Born March 18th 1887
Violet Alberta Follick
   Born April 7th 1889
Walter Owen Follick
   Born July 21st 1891
Richard Allen Follick
   Born March 22nd 1894
Edmund & Edna Follick
   Born August 17th 1899
Harriet Ellen Follick
   Born February 17th 1868
John William Follick
   Born February 20th 1862

Harriet Ellen Follick
Died July 11th 1905

Walter Ervin Follick
Born July 21, /18.91.
Cenboro Ont Nov, 4, 1972
Clara Louisa Mitchell
Born Aug 28/1893.
St Cathaines Ont Died Nov. 27, 1956
Dorathy Irine Follick
Born Sept 24/1911
N Tonawanda NY Nov 13, 1966
Thelma Florence Follick
N Tonawanda NY born Feb 24
Elmer Frederick Follick
Niagara Fall NY Born Feb 24/1917
Walter Ervin Follick Jr.
Born Jan 15/35
Delevan N.Y.

Bible of John William Follick & Harriet Ellen Rew's family.

91

Mary Follick wife of Jonathan Russell & Violet Vollick wife of Harold Theal

Hannah Haun, wife of Jacob Follick

David Follick
1860-1921

Hannah Haun wife of Jacob Follick with Bertha Follick Gifford & son Blake

John Vetor & Esther Follick

Smith Follick & Mary Jane Varey

Clarence Follick, Parry Sound ON

George Alexander Follick
1832-1911

William Freeman Dayton & Mary Jane Follick with children

Walter E. Follick & family   Harriet & Louise Follick

Ed & Mettie Warren 1891
Dunnville Ontario

Matthys Follick>Rachel Follick
married James Warren

Courtesy of Dale Van Alstine

John William Follick

Isabel Follick wife of Frank Dayton

FRANK & ISABEL DAYTON FAMILY

ville in his 75th year.

A young man named Bowins drove up to the residence of Peter Follick, Canfield, to drive him to the polls. They waited for a freight train to pass the M.C.R. crossing on the Stage Road, and then went ahead. When crossing the second track they were struck by a special express, running 50 miles per hour. Mr. Follick was killed, but Mr. Bowins escaped uninjured.

Mrs. S. Marshall, mother of Mrs.

Peter Follick 1844-1899
s/o Peter Follick
& Ellen Crane

tack of erysipelas.

A very serious accident occurred at the railway crossing a mile and a half west of this village. Peter Follick and Bert Bowins, failing to see the train coming, were run into by an express, the former instantly killed, and the latter slightly injured, but not seriously. The horse was killed and the buggy broken to pieces.

One Man Killed, His Companion Badly Injured.

Michigan Central Train Runs Into a Rig at a Crossing.

Canfield, Ont., Jan. 2.—About ten o'clock this morning Peter Vollick and Bert Bowins, while crossing the railway track one mile west of Canfield, in a covered buggy, were struck by the Michigan Central express, killing Vollick instantly, horse and buggy being demolished. Bowins escaped with slight injuries. Vollick was a farmer, aged about 55, and unmarried. The train was going at a high rate of speed.

Another of the Same.

Dunnville, Ont., Jan. 2.—Peter Follick was killed this evening while attempting to cross the M. C. R. tracks in Moulton. A freight was standing across the road, and when it backed out of the way Follick drove on the track, not seeing the fast express approaching on the other track, which struck the waggon, killing him instantly.

NANCY FOLLICK DIES AFTER NOBLE LIFE

(Special Correspondence.)

DINGLE, June 16.—Funeral services were held here recently in the ward meetinghouse, over the remains of Nancy Follick, who died at Montpelier, Idaho, May 19, 1909, of heart failure. Bishop Samuel Humpherys presided. Consoling and comforting remarks were made by Elders F. M. Dayton, H. Oakey, and Bishop Humphreys.

NANCY FOLLICK.

The funeral was well attended. A large cortege followed the remains to the cemetery. Mrs. Follick was born Sept. 8, 1828, at Elizabeth, Leers county, Canada. She was married to George A. Follick, April 15, 1857. She moved with her husband and parents to Iowa, the following year and crossed the plains with ox teams to Denver, Colo., in 1862. Five years later, during the perilous Indian troubles, she rode a stage coach from Denver to Tooele City, Utah, bringing three children with her, and joining her parents at that place. Her husband remained in Colorado. He followed to Tooele a year later.

They lived in Utah until 1879, when they moved to Dingle Idaho, where, with the exception of a temporary move, they have since resided. She leaves a husband, 77 years of age, a twin brother, James Parker, of Yerington, Nev., a younger brother, William Parker, of Tooele City, Utah, a half-brother, S. M. Elliott of Port Elgin, Canada, and a half-brother, Abel Parker, living in Nevada, five children, 33 grandchildren and eight great-grandchildren. She was a sincere Latter-day Saint, and at the time of her death, was acting treasurer of the Dingle Relief Society, which position she had held for about eight years. Much of the time of her closing years was spent in deeds of charity and for the betterment of mankind. The five surviving children are: Mrs. F. M. Dayton, Dingle Idaho; Mr. David Follich, Montpelier, Idaho; Mrs. William F. Dayton, Dingle, Idaho; Mrs. Roy George, Montpelier, Idaho; Mrs. John R. George of Raymond, Idaho.

Deseret evening news. (Great Salt Lake City [Utah]), 19 June 1909.
Chronicling America: Historic American Newspapers. Lib. of Congress.

ANOTHER HUNTING ACCIDE

The Salt Lake herald. (Salt Lake City [Utah], 15 Oct. 1889. *Chronicling America: Historic American Newspapers.* Lib. of Congress.

Abel Follick 1877-1889

Abel Follick Fatally Shot by Young Dayton.

A very sad and fatal accident oc
on Sunday last, shortly before su
near the settlement of Dingledell.
boys named Robert Stephens, Abel l
and Oliver Dayton, after attending S
school that day, went in the bottoms
the settlement, which abounds in
sloughs and ponds, to shoot ducks.
were sitting on the banks of one of
ponds when it was Oliver Dayton's
shoot the next ducks; he took the gu
as the ducks they saw coming towa
pond did not come within range, l
ered the gun which, it seems, wou
stay cocked about once out of three
and, when about one foot from t
shoulder of young Follick, went
charge passing through the shoulde
and lodging in his chest. He was coi
to his home in Dingledell by Boyd V
who was going by at the time with
of wood, and Dr. Hoover was sent fo
he being on the opposite side of the
did not reach there until 11:30 p.m
found the boy dead, having lived bu
minutes.

Justice Smedley, of Paris precinc
moned a coroner's jury and held an ii
The following gentlemen compos
jury: George Humphrey, Samuel H
rey, H. A. Dayton, Frank Dayton,
W. Sparks and Heber Smedley.
hearing all the evidence in the cas
rendered a verdict to the effect tha
Follick came to his death accident.
gun shot wound from a defective
the hands of Oliver Dayton; that tl
Dayton had no knowledge as to the c
of the gun, and that no blame could
tached to him.—Montpelier *Observer.*

Tooele, May 12.—The district court has adjourned and the jury has been discharged for the term. Edward W. Rodeback was charged with adultery with one Martha Follick. Mr. Rodeback had married one of George Follick's daughters, and in due time a baby came to bless their union. Because of the meager financial condition of Mr. Rodeback, George Follick furnished him a home for himself and wife. Mr. Follick and his family nursed Mr. Rodeback's wife through a long illness, and while they were thus doing Mr. Rodeback is charged with repaying the kindness of the family by accomplishing the ruin of the youngest daughter, Martha, a girl of 16 years.

At the trial Mr. Rodeback was represented by Messrs. Hutchison and Baker, who made an able defense. The case was given to the jury at about 10 o'clock. It took the jury about 30 minutes to agree upon a verdict of "guilty as charged." Sentence will be passed on June 1.

In the case of Thomas J. Bryan vs. the Mercur Gold Mininb and Milling company the jury gave plaintiff a verdict for $8,000.

The Salt Lake herald. (Salt Lake City [Utah]), 13 May 1897. *Chronicling America: Historic American Newspapers*. Lib. of Congress.

FOR ADULTERY.

Edward W. Rodeback Sent Up For Two Years.

Tooele, Utah, June 1.—This morning Judge Cherry passed sentence upon Edward W. Rodeback, who was convicted upon a charge of adultery, at the regular May session of the district court. The sentence was for a term of two years, at hard labor, in the penitentiary.

Decoration Day was appropriately

The Salt Lake herald. (Salt Lake City [Utah]), 02 June 1897. *Chronicling America: Historic American Newspapers*. Lib. of Congress.

A very sudden death took place near Dunnville at the home of J. Warren on Feb. 5th, 1918, of Jesse Malam Follick, aged 75 years, 5 months and 29 days. He was laid at rest in the Moote Settlement burying ground beside his late wife, Isabella Jones (nee Follick). He left to mourn his loss two daughters and two sons, as follows: Mrs. John Durham of Beamsville, Mrs. Samuel Smith of Dunnville, Mathias of Stratford and George of Buffalo, N.Y.

Chronicle Gazette 1919. P 9

Endnotes

[1] Transcribed and Indexed by Arthur C. M. Kelly, Baptism Record St. Paul's Lutheran Church 1728-1800, (1977), Schoharie Lutheran #810. Parents Isac Falk, Maria. Child Sturm born 17 Feb 1765, bpt 19 Feb 1765 Wit Nehrich Werner, Catharina Zahen.

[2] UCLP #87 entered in Land Book A page 95

[3] MG 19 A3 vol 41. NAC holds the private papers of Charles Askin a captain of the 2nd Regiment of the Lincoln Militia. Charles' papers are not microfilmed and are in very fragile condition.

[4] Township of Thorold, 1793-1967 : centennial project of the Township of Thorold Author: Michael, Betti Publisher: Toronto: Armath Associates, 1967

[5] Courtesy of Eric Bowler ebowler@interlog.com

[6] Family bible copied by William Oxford, Midland Ontario

[7] Welland County Death Certificates, Jacob Follack [sic] died 23 July 1887 Welland Co

[8] Family bible copied by William Oxford, Midland Ontario

[9] Christian Messenger, V 4, 10 Aug. 1865. FOLLACK. Died at her residence in Canboro on 26th ult., Rachael Follack, wife of Mr. Jacob Follack in the 56th year of her age.

[10] Christian Messenger, V. 5, 29 Nov. 1866. FOLLICK-WAY. On 24th Oct by Rev E. Chesney, Jacob Follick, esq to Mrs. Christina Way, relict of the late Rev. D. Way all of Canboro

[11] French816@aol.com, *Noreen French correspondence*, (October 2001), "Electronic," Noreen says she saw this in a Family Bible.

[12] 1851 Census Canborough, Add 2 years to the ages given in 1851 census. It was taken in 1852

[13] 1851 Census Canborough

[14] Petition of widow Gittie on his death, Matthias dying intestate..

[15] Ontario, Canada Deaths, 1869-1932 Haldimand 1900, Gittie VOLLICK, June 2, 1900. Age 84 years Lived at Conc 3 Canboro. Born Canboro. Baptist. Died of old age

[16] Ontario, Canada Deaths, 1869-1932 Haldimand 1900, James White d 2 Aug 1900, 83 years old, married, living Alder/n St, b Ireland, 6 months of kidney trouble, Episcopalian. Dunnville Haldimand Co

[17] Ontario, Canada Deaths, 1869-1932 Haldimand 1882, Canboro Tp: George Follick, died 20 Nov. 1882, 68 years old, farmer born Ontario. Isaac Follick of Canboro was informant. Methodist. No cause of death recorded

[18] Family bible copied by William Oxford, Midland Ontario

[19] Welland County Death Certificates, Jacob Follack [sic] died 23 July 1887 Welland Co.

[20] Family bible copied by William Oxford, Midland Ontario

[21] Christian Messenger, V 4, 10 Aug. 1865. FOLLACK. Died at her residence in Canboro on 26th ult., Rachael Follack, wife of Mr. Jacob Follack in the 56th year of her age

[22] Christian Messenger, V. 5, 29 November. 1866. FOLLICK-WAY. On 24th Oct by Rev E. Chesney, Jacob Follick, esq to Mrs. Christina Way, relict of the late Rev. D. Way all of Canboro

[23] French816@aol.com, *Noreen French correspondence*, (October 2001), "Electronic," Note. Noreen says she saw this in a Family Bible

[24] Film #0349211 p. 13

[25] LDS film # 0,349,273 NAC film # C-1028

[26] http://www.ancientancestors.net/F226/F226964.htm

[27] FHL Film 1375890 NAC C-13254 Dist 144 SubDist G Div 2 Page 22 Family 131

[28] Family History Library Microfilm: 1030057

[29] Family bible copied by William Oxford, Midland Ontario

[30] Marriage Date: 1 Aug 1874 Marriage Place: Straffordville Registration Number: 001656 Archives of Ontario Microfilm: 13

[31] Family bible copied by William Oxford, Midland Ontario

[32] Family bible copied by William Oxford, Midland Ontario

[33] Ontario, Canada Deaths, 1869-1932 Haldimand 1912, Father Jacob Follick, Mother Rachel Smith, living House of Refuge in Dunnville, born May 24, 1828 died November. 12, 1912, died of heart failure, has been ailing for years single, labourer

[34] 1851 Census Canborough, Add 2 years to the ages given in 1851 census. It was taken in 1852

[35] Ontario Deaths: Male, 71 years old, living Lot 71, Conc. 3, Canboro. Farmer, married, died of paralysis had for 4 months

[36] 1851 Census Canborough.

[37] Film 0349211 p. 39:

[38] FHL Film 1375890 NAC C-13254 Dist 144 SubDist F Div 1 Page 23 Family 122

[39] LDS film # 0,349,273 NAC film # C-1028

[40] FHL Film 1375890 NAC C-13254 Dist 144 SubDist F Div 2 Page 4 Family 21

[41] Ontario, Canada Deaths, 1869-1932 Haldimand 1920, Sarah Lattimore, died at Locke St. Female, German origin, widow, 85 years 2 mos 26 days old, born Canboro Tp Aug 15, 1835. Father Peter Follick born Pennsylvania USA, mother Mary Labatte, born Quebec, Informant Mr. [sic] R. N. Killens, daughter, buried Dunnville November. 13, 1920, Died November. 10, 1920 of Arteriosclerosis had for several years. Contributory causes Cardiac failiure and hemoplagea

[42] Haldimand County Marriage Registrations, Latimore Francis, 25, Moulton, Canada, s/o Robert & Susan, married 16 Dec 1862 Sarah Folick, 22, Dunnville, Canada, d/o Peter & Mary

[43] : Ontario, Canada Deaths, 1869-1932 Haldimand 1906, Dunnville, Haldimand Co: Francis Lattimore, night watchman, born Haldimand Co. Dropped dead. Residence Chestnut St. Married, 69 years old

[44] Haldimand Co. N Cayuga Tp Andrew Follick, German origin, 85 years old, married, born Haldimand Co., farmer, lived 15 years present residence. Doctor in Dunnville, Informant George Bloomfield, brother in law, of Waterford. Buried Windecker Cemetery, N. Cayuga on 27 Feb. 1925 Died Feb 24 of Arterior Sclerosis and Cerebral Hemorraghe

[45] #003967-86 (Haldimand Co): Andrew FOLLICK, 38, farmer, Canboro, same, s/o Peter & Ellen, married Elizabeth STEVENS, 37, Niagara twp., same, d/o Alexander & Mary Margaret, witn: Maria SMITH of Dunnville & William WALKER of Rainham, 20 April 1886 at Dunnville.

[46] Haldimand County Death Registrations, Canboro. Elizabeth Follick, 50 yeas old, living Darling Road, 3rd Concession, farmer's wife, born Homer Ontario died of heart disease had for 8 months. Informant Andrew Follick. Methodist

[47] Name: Nancy Bloomfield Spouse Name: Andrew Folick Marriage Date: 3 November 1897 Marriage Place: Hagersville Registration Number: 006254 Archives of Ontario Microfilm: 92

[48] Peter Follick #010457, died Jan 2 1899, 55 years old, residence Darling Road, single, farmer, born Canboro, killed in Railway accident

[49] Petition of widow Gittie on his death, Matthias dying intestate

[50] Ontario, Canada Deaths, 1869-1932 Haldimand 1900, Gittie VOLLICK, June 2, 1900. Age 84 years Lived at Conc 3 Canboro. Born Canboro. Baptist. Died of old age

[51] LDS film # 0,349,273 NAC film # C-1028

[52] FHL Film 1375890 NAC C-13254 Dist 144 SubDist F Div 2 Page 13 Family 67

[53] Death Certificate, Gardener, living Park Lot 74, Park St Sarawah. Father Frederic, mother's

name not known but born Germany. Informant Jacob Walters, Brookhohm [?] His Dr was in Owen Sound

[54] Ontario, Canada Deaths, 1869-1932 Haldimand 1900, James White d 2 Aug 1900, 83 years old, married, living Alder/n St, b Ireland, 6 months of kidney trouble, Episcopalian. Dunnville Haldimand Co

[55] Ontario, Canada Deaths, 1869-1932 Haldimand 1882, Canboro Tp: George Follick, died 20 November. 1882, 68 years old, farmer born Ontario. Isaac Follick of Canboro was informant. Methodist. No cause of death recorded.).

[56] LDS film # 0,349,273 NAC film # C-1028

[57] FHL Film 1375890 NAC C-13254 Dist 144 SubDist F Div 2 Page 11 Family 56

[58] Family bible copied by William Oxford, Midland Ontario

[59] Death Certificate, #015332, Catherine Mellick, 86 years old, born Canboro, died Moulton, widow, father Jacob Follick, mother Rachel Smith, died of old age.

[60] FHL Film 1375890 NAC C-13254 Dist 144 SubDist E Div 1 Page 40 Family 212

[61] FHL Film 1375890 NAC C-13254 Dist 144 SubDist F Div 2 Page 6 Family 31

[62] Family bible copied by William Oxford, Midland Ontario

[63] *Ontario Register 1780-1870*, (CD #204), "CD-ROM," Vol. VII, Christian Guardian. Marriage Notices 1858 (20 Jan 1858 p 32) On 24th ult, at the Wesleyan Parsonage, Smith F. Follick and Mary Jane Narey [sic] both of Canboro. Rev P Ker Also in Haldimand Co. Marriages & Burials, 1851-65

[64] Ontario, Canada Deaths, 1869-1932 Haldimand 1914, Mary Jane Follick, Age 77 born Lockport New York, died Oct 15, 1914 died in Canboro. Father's name VERY. Cause of death - heart. Informant Sydney Follick.

[65] FHL Film 1375890 NAC C-13254 Dist 144 SubDist F Div 2 Page 5 Family 27

[66] Microfilm T-6470 Subdistrict: b-1 Page 1 Schedule 1

[67] Microfilm Roll Number: M1478_21

[68] : 1871 census Norfolk Co. Middleton Tp

[69] *Melick Cemetery, Canboro Ontario*, (courtesy of Keith Topp, August 1994).

[70] Name: Henry Edwin Follick Marriage Date: 22 Jan 1894 Marriage Place: Niagara Falls Registration Number: 012376

[71] *Melick Cemetery, Canboro Ontario*, (courtesy of Keith Topp, August 1994)

[72] 1871 census Norfolk Co. Middleton Tp

[73] Ontario, Canada Deaths, 1869-1932 Haldimand 1885, Robert Vernin Follick. Baptist. Died of Scarlet Fever, 14 years old. Born Canboro. died 19 Feb 1855

[74] Family bible copied by William Oxford, Midland Ontario

[75] Ontario, Canada Deaths, 1869-1932 Elgin 1917, William Follick died d Oct. 10, 1917, 82 years old, widower, born 1835, died at Elgin House of Industry in Southwald Tp, Retired, father Jacob Follick. died instantly of cerebral softening and apoplexy. Informant George A. Allen of Alymer

[76] copied by William Oxford, Midland Ontario, *Follick Family bible.*

[77] FHL Film 1375902 NAC C-13266 Dist 163 SubDist D Div 2 Page 16 Family 80

[78] a-2 Page 1 Details: Schedule 1 Microfilm T-6464

[79] 19169-03 (Welland Co)

[80] Family bible copied by William Oxford, Midland Ontario

[81] FHL Film 1375890 NAC C-13254 Dist 144 SubDist F Div 1 Page 25 Family 133

[82] T623 Roll 1032 p. 201

[83] T624 Roll 946 p. 40

[84] Family bible copied by William Oxford, Midland Ontario)

[85] Pleasanton Township Cemetery, Manistee, Michigan, Robert H. 1848 – 1911.

http://www.rootsweb.com/~usgenweb/mi/tsphoto/manistee/pleasanton.htm

[86] #001639-74 (Elgin Co): Robert H. FOLLOCK, 26, farmer, Camber Ont., South Dorchester, s/o Jacob & Rachel, married Mary CHAMBERS, 22, South Dorchester, same, d/o Daedalus & Jane, witn: William FOLLOCK & William APPLEFORD, both of S. Dorchester, 5 July 1874 at Mapleton, Yarmouth twp

[87] Pleasanton Township Cemetery, Manistee, Michigan, Mary 1854 -1891. http://www.rootsweb.com/~usgenweb/mi/tsphoto/manistee/pleasanton.htm

[88] Courtesy of Sharon Kirk October 2007

[89] From Sharon Kirk October 2007

[90] Pleasanton Township Cemetery, Manistee, Michigan, Cortland 1876 -1957. http://www.rootsweb.com/~usgenweb/mi/tsphoto/manistee/pleasanton.htm

[91] Family bible copied by William Oxford, Midland Ontario

[92] Ontario, Canada Deaths, 1869-1932 Haldimand 1921, Jesse Follick, father Jacob, mother not known, 70 years 5 mos 8 days old died 7 feb 1921. Retired farmer, living current address 10 years, Informant Mrs. J. Follick of Dunnville, wife. buried Melick Cemetery, Canboro. Died of pneumonia Feb 7, 1921

[93] Ontario, Canada Deaths, 1869-1932 Haldimand 1926, Dunnville. Eliza Winne Follick. Father George Sporbeck born Canboro Ontario. Mother Mary McFadden born Ireland. Living 14 years current residence Helena St N. in Dunnville. Widow, 71 years 1 month 28 days old. Informant George Follick of Hamilton Ontario, son. Buried Canboro Aug 10, 1926. Died of Senility and pneumonia

[94] FHL Film 1375904 NAC C-13268 Dist 167 SubDist B Div 2 Page 13 Family 64

[95] Frances Edgar Follick 2 Jul 1877 Male Middlesex Jesse E Follick Eliza Shawback

[96] Father Jesse Edwin Follick b Canboro, mother Eliza Spurlock b N Cayuga. certified by Jesse Follick N Cayuga, died of Chronic Endoearithis of 6 years duration.

[97] George Jacob Follick 4 Jun 1884 Male Middlesex Jesse Follick Eliza Sperback.);

[98] Accident where death occurred - Curtin [Curtis?] Follick, killed at Dunnville, Ontario, July 5, 1937, Canadian National Railway

[99] *Death Registration*, #035456, buried Overholt Cemetery, Pt. Colborne, Ontario

[100] *Marriage Registration at Ontario Archives*, # 003329, Jacob Root, 36, of Sherbrook to Cinthia Vollick, 35, of Canboro d/o Mathew and Guitty on Feb 13, 1877. Also: 003329-1877 (Haldimand Co.) Jacob ROOT, 36, Widower, Farmer, Sherbrook, same, s/o John & Hannah, married Cinthia VOLLICK, 35, Canboro, same, d/o Mathew & Gertty, witn: James H. WHITE of Seneca & James P. WILLOUGHBY of Caledonia, 13 Feb 1877 at Caledonia

[101] Birth Registration Ontario Archives, #208364

[102] Birth Registration Ontario Archives, #010645

[103] Haldimand County Death Registrations, Canboro: Jesse Malen Follic, 75 years old, died Feb. 5, 1918 in Canboro Tp. Born Canboro, labourer. Buried Moots Settlement Cemetery. widower. Father Methias Follick. Mother Gittie McLauchlin. Cause of death sudden Harmophlyia

[104] Ontario, Canada Deaths, 1869-1932 Kent 1899, Harvey H. VOLLICK June 28, 1899 at age 49 years Born in Ontario. Died of cerebral hemorraghe. Methodist. Residence Tillbury East

[105] WW1 Attestation Papers

[106] Commonwealth Graves Commission

[107] courtesy of <bobbyshobby@email.msn.com>, Phone Interview with Eleanor